MAZZAROTH

and the

BIRTH OF A NATION

Harry Golemon

Clovercroft Publishing

Mazzaroth and the Birth of a Nation

©2016 by Harry Golemon

Published by Clovercroft Publishing, Franklin, Tennessee

Published in association with Larry Carpenter of Christian Book Services, LLC of Franklin, Tennessee

Scripture is used from the New King James Version, © 1982 by Thomas Nelson, Inc. All rights reserved. Used by permission.

Edited by Gail Fallen

Cover Design by Suzanne Lawing

Interior Layout Design by Adept Content Solutions

ISBN: 978-1-942557-35-7

Printed in the United States of America

Contents

Appreciation

First and foremost, how can one properly begin to thank the Mystical, Spiritual Being, in which we can only gain a glimpse so miniscule that if the blink was any longer, containing it would be impossible; we would be on the brink of death.

I would like to thank God for his revealing of knowledge to me, for the still, soft voice guiding me on the paths. Even though I may have had an idea that was wrong, the research for this book actually showed me answers to other questions I was contemplating.

To my wife who tolerated my overly enthusiastic, overbearing hyper self, especially before she had a chance to drink her first sip of coffee. "I know where the stones go!"

To my two sons, Matthew and Mark, whom I hope to be able to show a truer meaning of those twinkling miracles in the night sky and to be better prepared when you ask me the question, "What's the meaning of those lights in the sky?"

To my Sunday school teacher, Randy, who unlocked my ability to study God's Word, gaining knowledge exponentially over a short period of time.

For my Bible study leader, Elmo, for listening to my theories, assisting me, and allowing me to bounce off ideas.

To the numerous people at church and strangers who were brave enough to listen to me explain what God had shown me in His Word.

To Heather, Bert, Laura, Craig, Charile, and my wife for proofreading.

To the IAU and NASA for publishing the data and allowing access to study the stars on an amateur level. May this book help those who want to study astronomy or be an astronomer in the future.

Foreword

"Then God said, 'Let there be light'; and there was light."

—Genesis 1:3 (New King James Version)

"He counts the number of the stars;

He calls them all by name.

Great is our Lord, and mighty in power;

His understanding is infinite."

—Psalms 147:4–5

Several years ago, on my way home late one evening, I happened to notice a small thunderstorm playing itself out over Sabine Lake, far to the south. Being a huge fan of lightning storms, I pulled over, got out, and stood by the road enjoying the light show in the far sky and the deep roll of distant thunder following long after each burst. Slowly, the storm seemed to drift farther south, the flashes of light dimmer and the thunder taking longer to seek me. Suddenly, a great flash of light bolted through the sky, reaching well over my head, as other bolts scattered to the horizons on the east and west. The clap was immediate, frightening, and much louder than any I had ever heard before. I crouched in startled fear as the bolts illuminated a MASSIVE thunderstorm now moving NORTH over my head, one whose tiny mischief at its far south edge didn't begin to hint at its true power. Soaking wet, huddled in my truck, shivering with spent adrenaline, I watched the storm rage about with more crashes and flashes. A verse of Scripture, unbidden by my conscience, drifted to mind:

"Indeed these are the mere edges of His ways, And how small a whisper we hear of Him! But the thunder of His power who can understand?"

—Job 26:14

Harry has managed to peel back one of those edges ever so slightly and has invited us along for the ride.

I first met Harry in a small group Bible study. He was quiet, reserved, almost shy, with a quick smile that lit up his face and a slight knowing grin in his eyes that hinted to "something" more. Over a few weeks, as the small group discussed the Word and its work in our lives, I discovered his unassuming demeanor veiled a deep intellect, inquisitive, tenacious, coupled with the discipline of an engineer. His questions (questions only, rarely declarative statements), indicated a quick and solid grasp of the subject and a desire for deeper or wider meaning, how it linked with other subjects, how what he had learned could lever open what he did not yet see. Watching him work it out made Bible study fun for me once again, and for that I am eternally grateful.

Then he happened upon a rather obscure phrase in the book of Job. Job has questioned God, His fairness, His justice, and His very judgment. In the middle of God's reply was this:

> "Can you bind the cluster of the Pleiades,
>
> Or loose the belt of Orion?
>
> Can you bring out Mazzaroth in its season?
>
> Or can you guide the Great Bear with its cubs?
>
> Do you know the ordinances of the heavens?
>
> Can you set their dominion over the earth?"
>
> —Job 38:31–33

What in the world is a Mazzaroth?? To paraphrase Doyle, "The game was afoot"; the hunt was on.

What follows is a result of that hunt. In it, Harry peels back an edge, peeking a bit beyond the "mere edges," and discovers the possibility that God really is "in control" . . . in control beyond "all we can ask or think." God is not just in control of my every circumstance, but in control of the very universe down to the placement of the patterns recognizable to ancient peoples. Typical of Harry, he doesn't just hand you this revelation; that would be too easy, and where's the fun in that? He merely asks questions . . . baiting you to consider . . . consider that God is not a distant God, aloof, detached from His creation; consider that He is not only here and now and interested in our lives minute by minute, but that He was there and interested in showing Himself in every aspect of creation, from the budding of a flower to the very arrangement of the stars in the heavens. He is everywhere and every when. The psalmist wrote:

"Where can I go from Your Spirit?

Or where can I flee from Your presence?

If I ascend into heaven, You are there;

If I make my bed in hell, behold, You are there."

—Psalms 139:7–8

Harry sends us chasing the Mazzaroth into the very heavens and, like the psalmist, we discover that God was already there.

Now there are at least two ways to read this book. One, grab a pencil and a pad, take copious notes, follow the same research, slog the same paths, and ask the same questions. For some of us, that's fun. Or two, just read and let Harry's questions percolate, simmer. Which way you choose is up to you, but do so seeking Him; seek to find Him even in the specks of light filling the night sky and He will be found.

"I love those who love me, And those who seek me diligently will find me."

—Proverbs 8:17

"So I say to you, ask, and it will be given to you; seek, and you will find; knock, and it will be opened to you. For everyone who asks receives, and he who seeks finds, and to him who knocks it will be opened."

—Luke 11:9–10

—Randy Culp

Introduction

"Stop. I do not care what others saw, I want to know what you see."

As I began my initial study for this treasure you now hold in your hand, I was reading Scriptures, and pouring through all kinds of reference materials, when I heard the above message in my head. I hope to never forget the message I heard that day, for I considered it a Divine message, a message changing the way I read and study the Bible. A message I heed, which led me to discover mysteries in the Bible.

You are holding a product of proof of a statement from the wisest, most humble servant this planet has ever known.

"Ask, and it will be given to you; seek, and you will find; knock, and it will be opened to you."

—Matthew 7:7 NKJV

The work, dedication, study, prayer, and patience were not easy, and many hours were spent asking questions, seeking answers, and knocking for the knowledge of truth. I do not feel I am 100 percent correct and accurate in all my interpretations, but I want to show the small results and gain your interest in studying the Word of God on your own. In my blunders, I hope you conduct your own studies, allowing God to reveal Himself to you.

The Bible was written for you and for me. It speaks to us individually with the hope of capturing a small glimpse of the Most Divine. The main purpose of this book is to show you the methods I took in studying an odd word found in the Bible and pique your interest in reading the Bible. This one word opened many doors of understanding, even knowledge, for which I was not searching.

The message I was given early in this study forced me to pick apart items in the Bible using my skillsets, with which the Lord has blessed me. Of course, references were used in the nature of science and historical research, but I refrained from using others' interpretations of Scripture until I had exhausted my own. A practice I still adhere to. Doing the work myself showed me things others had not seen, and it will show you things I did not see. This is the mystery of the Bible as a living, breathing book; it speaks differently to us all, afresh from day to day.

Another purpose of this book is to show how God knew the end from the beginning when He began creation. I hope to show a part of His creation in a new light so that you have a better appreciation of the nighttime scene. The universe was created for us so that we may look at the wonders of the heavens and see the mighty handiwork of the Creator.

A writer I studied in high school, Ralph Waldo Emerson, poet, essayist, and transcendentalist, wrote of his appreciation of creation in chapter 1 of his essay "Nature." I could have not said it any better.

"One might think the atmosphere was made transparent with this design, to give man, in the heavenly bodies, the perpetual presence of the sublime. Seen in the streets of cities, how great they are! If the stars should appear one night in a thousand years, how would men believe and adore; and preserve for many generations the remembrance of the city of God which had been shown! But every night come out these envoys of beauty, and light the universe with their admonishing smile."[1]

The Mazzaroth

"Can you bind the sweet influences of the Pleiades
or loose the bands of Orion?
Can you bring forth **Mazzaroth** in its season?
Or can you guide the Great Bear with its cubs?
Do you know the ordinances of the heavens?
Can you set the dominion over the earth?"

—Job 38: 31–34 NKJV (emphasis mine)

I awake to start the day, soon realizing it is four in the morning. I lay back in bed and ponder for the next hour, drifting in and out of sleep. As the clock gets closer to five or shortly thereafter, I get out of bed and walk to my sons' room. Turning on the lights, I wake up my oldest son, Matthew. He sleeps on the top section of the bunk bed. His younger brother, Mark, in the bottom section. With eyes half shut from the overhead light blinding him, he holds out his arms in his usual request, "Carry me." I lift up my arms. He groggily moves to the edge, grabbing his "blanky" on the way, and slides into my arms as I lift him up and out of bed. I carry him to the living room and lay him down on the couch.

After a few minutes, we go outside to the patio garden to look at the stars, talk, listen to music, and read. It is fall, and looking into the eastern sky, we see the belt of Orion. Some mornings, we would catch the International Space Station going by overhead, but mainly we are outside to observe the magnitude of stars as the last fleeting hours of night are passing.

My knowledge of the stars at this point in my life was very limited. Growing up I knew the Little and Big Dipper and called Jupiter Venus for many, many years.

One morning, my son points out a cluster of stars named the Pleiades, calling it the Little Dipper. "I see it, there is the Little Dipper," he exclaims. We have a brief and typical son to dad argument, so I get a star map to show him it is actually the constellation Pleiades he has spotted.

Out of curiosity, I ask, "Are stars mentioned in the Bible?" Opening a Bible application, we ran a search on stars and found several references.

"I wonder if Orion is in the Bible," I ask playfully. To my surprise, Orion was mentioned three times.

"Which maketh Arcturus, **Orion**, and Pleiades, and the chambers of the south."

—Job 9:9 King James Version (emphasis mine)

"Canst thou bind the sweet influences of Pleiades, or loose the bands of **Orion**?"

—Job 38:31 (emphasis mine)

"Seek him that maketh the seven stars and **Orion** . . ."

—Amos 5:8

Reading through the chapters where these three verses are found, I came across a word that I would have normally ignored. In Job chapter 38, I found an interesting word, *Mazzaroth*. I began looking through the list of constellations and stars on my star map. I did not find the Mazzaroth in the search, but the Mazzaroth was in the skies.

Entering my amateur study of astronomy, I knew very little about stars and constellations, but learned at an early age about the planets in elementary school and from a book my mother had purchased for me one Christmas. Growing up, I had access to my father's telescope, but I did not understand what I was viewing in the eyepiece. The little bright objects in the night sky increased slightly, and from an entertainment perspective of a young boy, the fun lasted for about ten minutes.

Beginning my study on the Mazzaroth, I purchased some star location software for my tablet and began looking for the stars mentioned in the Bible. As I panned across the nighttime sky, I noticed the software drew pictures over groups of stars, forming constellations. My son and I would look at the different drawings, and occasionally, he would wrest the tablet away from me to search for the drawings that appealed to him.

In case you may not be familiar with the term "constellation," the Merriam-Webster dictionary defines it as a group of stars that form a particular shape in the sky and has been given a name.[2] The origin of the word "constellation" is from Middle English *constellacioun* and from Late Latin *constellatio*. Constellations are also the configuration of stars at one's birth.

Constellations are recognizable patterns formed by connecting a group of stars with lines to create the likeness of a person, animal, or object, like a Connect the Dot game. Look at the following illustration; what do you see?

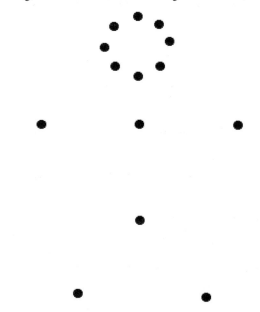

Do you see a circle, a line, and a triangle? A stick person? A flower and a vase? Something else?

The answer is not limited. It is whatever your imagination makes it out to be. The same goes with star patterns. There are many, many stars, and connecting the dots can lead to an unlimited number of patterns. When viewing the constellations with the naked eye, I would have come up with different objects than those appearing on the screen of my tablet.

As my interest in the stars grew, my oldest son, thinking of his dad, purchased a book from the school book fair on the constellations.

The book identified several patterns in the night sky and provided mythological stories behind the stars. We both read through the book, yet I found myself wanting to withdraw, for these stories were the Greek interpretation on the purpose of the patterns in the night sky. Having recently found some of the constellations in the Bible, I knew the Greek stories were written much later and did not have the same intentions.

A feeling of remorse came over me. I began to sense our history and society may have diluted and polluted the purpose of those bright lights in the night sky. By telling the mythological stories to my sons, it would also hinder a purer appreciation of the twinkling lights and the One who created them. Even the names given to those constellations in the Bible were translated to English from the mythological names identified by the Greeks.

The onset of seeing Orion in the Bible puzzled me, so I began to research the historical naming of the stars and locate the name for the Mazzaroth. Studying the identification, grouping, and naming of the stars throughout the documented history of ancient civilizations, I learned even today we continue to use the same pattern, and in some cases, the same identification they once observed.

For example, the Greeks identified the stars making up the constellation of Orion as a giant huntsman, with various interesting tales. The Chukchi, a Siberian tribe, drew out an archer,[3] and the Egyptians, around the twenty-fourth century BC, deified this constellation with Osiris, having the appearance of an Egyptian god holding a staff. The earliest civilization to emerge, the Sumerians around 3100 BC, identified the constellation of Orion as the Faithful Shepherd,[4] and finally, the ancient Hebrews may have identified Orion with Nimrod, the mighty hunter before God.

From this brief study I learned the constellation we call Orion historically had been identified similarly to a person-like figure, but with different intentions. Being inspired, I now have a different, maybe purer interpretation I can relay to my sons when we are outside during the nighttime, gazing upon the radiance of Nimrod, or a Faithful Shepherd.

As this study progressed, I began to tie other constellations to biblical references, which was the beginning to deeply studying the Bible, seeking and allowing God to open the doors of knowledge, and to become scholarly—

a historian, a geographer, chronologist, amateur astronomer, and ancient word linguistic. Early on, I did not grasp how these would tie together and be instrumental to understanding Scripture and unlocking some of the mysteries in the Bible.

As I conducted historical research, I was amazed how ancient civilizations, thousands of miles apart, some separated by oceans and seas, identified the same grouping and similar patterns for the stars. As seen in the previous example, there are multiple ways one can connect the dots, yet these ancient civilizations used the same stars and patterns. Was this grouping and identification from an original, single source? Was it Divine or used to hinder Divinity?

As I continued studying the history and naming of the stars, I found there was a lack of structure, and as methods improved nearing the twentieth century, we were discovering and naming more and more stars. Due to the advancement of discovery in astronomy, a group of astronomers in 1919 "promoted and safeguarded the science of astronomy"[5] by forming the International Astronomy Union (IAU). One of their purposes was to "facilitate cooperation in both science and education."[6] They also brought order to the naming of stars and constellations, and redefined a constellation as follows:

"In star maps it is common to mark line 'patterns' that represent the shapes that give the name to the constellations. However, the IAU defines a constellation by its boundary (indicated by sky coordinates) and not by its pattern and the same constellation may have several variants in its representation."[7]

This is a very good refinement of the definition, because it *frees* us to use our imagination as individuals to look up at the night sky and wonder, versus being confined to a set pattern. As I learned throughout this study, a grouping of stars can sometimes have more than one pattern, having different stories and relaying different messages.

Now that a constellation has been defined by Merriam-Webster and the IAU, I would like to show you where the constellations are directly mentioned in the Bible. Although translations vary, here is a list of the constellations with the Hebrew word provided, along with the verse where they are found.[8]

Hebrew	KJV	NKJV	Verses
Ayish (Ash)	Arcturus with his sons.	Great Bear with his cubs.	Job 9:9, 38:31
Kaciyl (Cesil)	Orion		Job 9:9, 38:31; Amos 5:8
Kaciyli (Cesili)	Constellations		Isaiah 13:10
Kimyah (Cimah)	Pleiades		Job 9:9, 38:31
Kimyah (Cimah)	Seven Stars		Amos 5:8

The number of things you can learn when conducting Bible studies is always fascinating. Scanning through the list of the constellations found in the Bible, I came across a hidden constellation in Isaiah 13:10. I was a little confused why the translators chose to use the general word "constellation" in place of *Kaciyl*, which I translated as Orion.

Knowing Orion is visible in the night sky during the events Isaiah proclaimed would allow us to know the time of the year the event takes (or took) place. Orion is currently visible in late summer to late spring, and I thought I had unlocked a mystery in the Bible.

After completing a version of the book for proofreading, I was in an airport in Germany where I came in contact with a couple who work as Bible translators for Wycliffe. I gave the Isaiah 13:10 verse to them as an example of a translation error; however, I was to receive a brief introduction into the Hebrew language.

They opened a Hebrew version of the Bible and read the chapter. After a few moments, the gentleman shared, "The word *Kaciyli* in Isaiah 13:10 is a plural form of the word, so the verse literally reads: 'the sun, moon and the "Orions" go dark'; therefore, the translators chose to use the word 'constellations.'"

Note that I added this section as an example of making an incorrect conclusion by using a reference to the Hebrew word without understanding the language.

Continuing on . . .

As I read through the verses where the constellations are directly mentioned, I looked for the constellations in the night sky with the aid of a star mapping software for my tablet. Due to their biblical references, these little bright lights in the night sky started taking on a different perspective. I soon realized I was sharing the same view of the night sky as those in the Bible did.

No matter how many ancient artifacts and documents had been lost, those same stars radiated throughout history, and tying a story to their perceived patterns was a way to give their message permanence. The stars are the one thing we cannot destroy.

If you do not have the convenience of a star mapping software on your tablet or smartphone, or you are reading this in the daytime, I will review where the constellations and stars in the Bible are found. To appreciate the handiwork of God, one does not need fancy equipment or even a telescope. The ancients did not have this luxury. Isaiah encourages us to just walk outside and admire creation and the Creator.

"Lift up your eyes on high, and behold who hath created these things, that bringeth out their host by number: he calleth them all by names by the greatness of his might, for that he is strong in power; not one faileth."

—Isaiah 40:26

Arcturus / The Great Bear

Let's begin with the first star found in the King James Bible: Arcturus with his sons. Arcturus is the brightest star in the northern part of the sky; it can be found by following the tail of Ursa Major, the handle of the Big Dipper. In the summertime in Texas, one can look directly up and find the reddish star. It connects with other stars to form the constellation, commonly called Bootes.

The following is a star map from the IAU's website.[9] Highlighted in white are the coordinates for the boundaries of the constellation Bootes. They have drawn light green lines, connecting the "dots," to form a commonly accepted pattern for Bootes. According to the scale in the bottom left, Arcturus is the largest star in this region, with a size rating of zero.

Scientists have found Arcturus is a red giant sun, approximately twenty-five times the size of our sun, and radiates more than one hundred times the light.

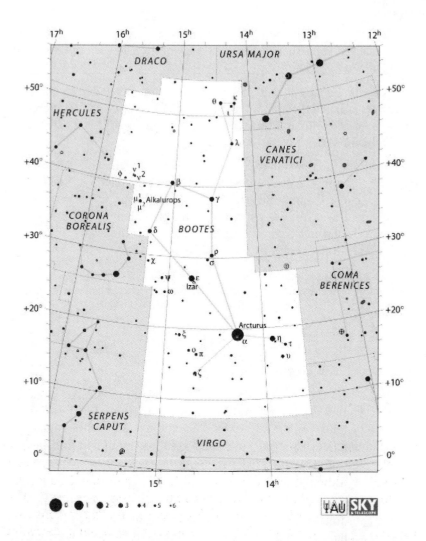

An alternative translation found in most newer Bible translations for the Hebrew word *Ayish* is the Ursa Major, sometimes called the Great Bear, and commonly called the Big Dipper. Like Arcturus, it is located in the northern sky and is a well-recognized constellation. Growing up, I learned this constellation as the Big Dipper, and during this study I learned the pattern is considered to make the outline of a bear.

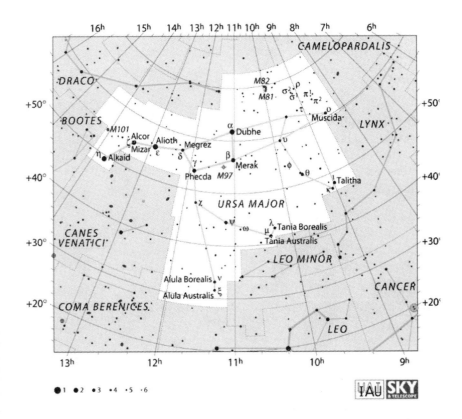

In the book of Job where this constellation is found, God is defining part of his role to Job, and He asks, "Can you guide the Great Bear with its cubs?" (Job 38:32). Although texts differ as to which group of stars God is referring to, an important point I understood in this translation is that **God acknowledges the stars form recognizable patterns, and He demonstrates He knows them by name. He not only acknowledges the patterns but also has placed them purposely for his purpose, and they move according to His will.**

Here is an interesting aspect about the Big Dipper. The ancients did not have the convenience of clocks like we have today. To tell the time at night, the Egyptians aligned two stars, sometimes the two pointer stars in the Big Dipper, when visible, with the North Pole star, Thuban. Connecting the dots created a clock with an hour hand.[10]

Employing the ancient Egyptians use of the Big Dipper, I believe that God may be asking Job if he can speed up time by moving the stars of this

constellation, or He is demonstrating His supreme sovereignty and dominion over not only all of creation, but of time itself.

Orion

Best viewed in the eastern sky in the month of January, I use Orion to help
identify the location of other constellations from late fall to early summer.
The ancient Hebrews may have called Orion *Nimrod*, the mighty hunter
before the Lord, found in Genesis. In the time of the Sumerian civilization,
they referred to this constellation as URU AN-NA, the Faithful Shepherd;[11]
others translate it as the True Shepherd of Anu.

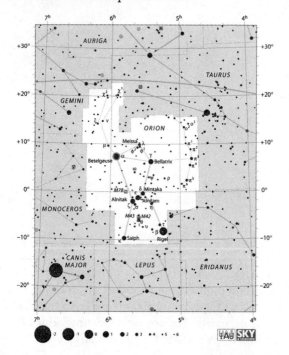

God asks Job if he can loosen the bands of Kaciyl, the three stars around
the waist, which we also call the belt of Orion. Researching the Hebrew
word Kaciyl, I found it is also used in the Bible to mean "fool." As from a
previous example of translating Kaciyl, I am not knowledgeable enough in
the Hebrew language to know if there was an identifier or article to distinguish between the uses, but I wanted to point out the different meanings
for Kaciyl.

Observing the stars making up this constellation, I imagine a warrior with
a bow and arrow.

Pleiades, the Seven Stars

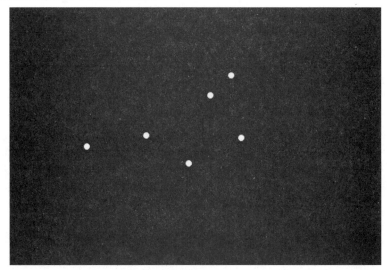

The Pleiades is a small group of six visible stars near the ecliptic above the back of Taurus the Bull, appearing like a miniature version of the Little Dipper. Depending on your age, you may see more than six stars; children have often been able to count ten.

Since the Pleiades is historically considered to have seven stars, various ancient stories were written on the disappearance of the seventh star. The disappearance is still a mystery, as the Sumerians, in 3100 BC, drew the Pleiades with seven stars. With the use of a telescope, one will find there are more than seven stars;[12] however, for practical purposes, I will only consider the stars visible to the ancients' naked eye.

God asked Job if he could bind the sweet influences of the Pleiades, for this constellation was once thought to guide the other constellations into the seasons. The Sumerians considered Pleiades as the "lead" constellation and the starting point in their star maps. According to *A Sumerian Observation of the Kofels Impact Event,*

"The Pleiades cluster was used by the Sumerians as the starting reference of angular measurements along the celestial equator and not the spring equinox used today."[13] The star we call Atlas was the precise zero point of the Sumerians.

Others, from a biblical standpoint, see the seven stars of the Pleiades to be the same seven stars found in Revelation. Thus, in their analogy, the sweet influences God refers to is of a future time when the Gospel is on Earth.[14]

This is Revelation's zero point, as the stars are very important at the start of John's book.

Twelve / Thirteen Constellations around Earth's Elliptic

Having reviewed the three constellations directly found in the Bible, I wondered if the remaining constellations had meanings other than those we commonly associate with Greek mythology.

There are currently eighty-eight constellations identified and named today, most defined by the ancient Greeks; however, the origin of the grouping and naming convention of the star patterns is not known. Some suggest Adam or his son Seth were the first astronomers, and the stars formed patterns to tell a message to the early inhabitants of Earth.

In the rise and destruction of civilizations, stones, scrolls, and any other form of records were destroyed. Great historical losses occurred with the burning of the Library of Alexandria and the Imperial Library of Constantinople. There is not much, if any, archeological proof of the exact origin of the naming of stars and constellations, but ancient paintings have been found in caves in Lascaux, France; in star maps on clay tablets used by the Sumerians; and in carvings on stone pillars in Syria.

Using the star maps on my tablet, my son would scan the nighttime scenery, looking for images of the constellations. When he found one of interest, the excitement of a seven-year-old would bubble forth, and he would have to show me what he found.

Increasing my knowledge of the constellations, I learned there were twelve main constellations circumventing the earth's elliptic, or position of the sun to the backdrop of stars as the earth orbits. These main constellations were identified by the Sumerians, and throughout time, these configuration of stars were placed on circular models for use in astronomy, cosmology, and astrology.

The Sumerians divided the night sky into eight visible sections and identified these twelve main constellations, which can be seen on a *planisphere*. These circular models of the constellations developed over time into a zodiac, which is thought to be an invention of the Akkadians during the time of Hammurabi around 1800 BC.[15]

When I first came across the word "Mazzaroth," I perceived it was a star or a constellation, since God used the word in the midst of other stars. The Mazzaroth, a *hapax legomenon*—a word or phrase only appearing once in a literary work, in this instance the Bible—led me on an adventure of biblical study and the writing of this book. It was a word that opened doors of understanding, knowledge, and a drive to know more about God.

To further my studies, I purchased Frances Rolleston's *Mazzaroth*, a book published in 1862, and read through it. By using the Hebrew root words for constellations found in the Old Testament, the book tied the constellations of the zodiac to the twelve tribes of Israel.[16] I cannot imagine how many hours she spent searching and researching, considering the limited technology of that time.

The book sent me searching in the night sky for the constellations she proposed were associated with the tribes. I began reading through the Bible, learning about the children for whom the tribes are named. I studied the birth and the life of each child and their blessing. This is when I saw a different method to identify the constellation with the tribe. I was reading Jacob's blessing for Dan when I realized he was describing the patterns he saw in the constellations, which we will see later in the book.

Being rather skeptical, I started reading through the biblical references and found myself in a deep study of God's Word. I took copious notes and completed study after study. I wanted to decipher and discover the intent behind God using the words "Mazzaroth" and "seasons," so the first step was to construct a timeline finding the period when Job lived. This would give me a time frame reference and the known influence of the civilizations of the time.

The Bible does not provide the exact age of Job, only that he lived 140 years after his test of perseverance. Using his age at death and estimating his age before his trials, I arrived at an approximate age of 200 years old when he died. Looking at life spans and periods of the early patriarchs, this placed Job between Noah and Abraham.

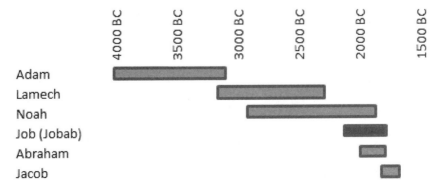

The Bible is so mysterious. When we are conducting one study, other studies and fascinating details often emerge. Working on the above timeline, I learned Noah was still alive during most of Abraham's life.

Near the end of this study, I realized Job may be the first written book of the Bible, predating the Law given by Moses. Reading through Job, you get a sense that the Law did not exist. I also began this timeline of what I considered the accepted start date for Adam, yet this would change the more I studied.

Furthering my study of the word "Mazzaroth," I read different Bible translations where this word is found. Some translated as "constellations" or "the twelve signs," but the *Complete Jewish Bible* translated Mazzaroth as "the constellations of the zodiac."[17] The zodiac? This puzzled me, for I always considered the signs of the zodiac to be part of the pagan column of the newspaper or something identified with serial killers! What is it doing in the Bible and why is God referencing it? (In conducting Bible studies, I find myself asking why a lot, just like a small child.)

On a three-hour flight for a mission trip to Guatemala, I had the fortunate opportunity to sit beside a graduate student of Rutgers University, who was from Haifa, Israel. During our conversations, I asked him about the word "Mazzaroth." He told me it was a dead-end word, and he did not know what it literally meant.

With continued research, I discovered the Mazzaroth was somehow tied to the twelve main constellations making up the zodiac. I reviewed the verse again, "the Mazzaroth in his **season**." Does this mean the season for the four natural seasons we experience on earth: spring, summer, fall, and winter? Does it mean an astronomical event that will happen, like the arrival of a comet?

Using online Bible study tools and applying the Strong numbers, the word "season," as found in Job 38:32, is from the Hebrew word *eth* and means the following:

> 1. Time
>   a. time (of an event)
>   b. time (usual)
>   c. experiences, fortunes
>   d. occurrence, occasion[18]

At first, I thought the word "season" used with the creation of the stars was the same Hebrew word; however, the word translated for season is *Mow'ed* and means the following:

1. appointed place, appointed time, meeting
2. appointed time (general)
3. sacred season, set feast, appointed season
   a. appointed meeting
   b. appointed place
   c. appointed sign or signal
   d. tent of meeting[19]

As this relates to my study on the Mazzaroth, some believe it may have been the ancient start of the zodiac; however, it could have been a star, constellation, or festival, where the identification or translation was lost. Not all Bible scholars and translations agree with the constellations or stars assigned in the book of Job, and they definitely do not agree with the word "Mazzaroth."

I did not choose the word "Mazzaroth" for part of the title of this book to necessarily decode the meaning of the word but to illustrate how this word was the starting point for this study, launching me to study the Bible in a more profound manner. In the end, this word took on a whole new and personal meaning to me, and I hope it gives you a new perspective for studying the Bible. For now, let's continue with the Jewish assumption—that the Mazzaroth was the start to the zodiac, or some representation thereof.

Today, we know the zodiac as being defined in twelve sections, identified with twelve main constellations. Approximately nine hundred years before the word "Mazzaroth" was uttered to Job, a clay tablet was found, accredited to the Sumerians. This tablet had eight observed divisions in the night sky and several stars and constellations mapped out.

The tablet has been dated to 3123 BC, about 350 years before the Great Flood, from the timeline I created. Scientists used computer software and the positions of the stars to calculate an accurate date for the star map of the clay tablet. Carbon 14 dating resulted in the clay tablet being created much later, making the clay tablet in the museum at Bristol an ancient carbon copy.

The tablet was copied and placed in the ancient Nineveh library of Ashurbanipal, and was later uncovered by Henry Layard in the nineteenth century. It now resides in a British Museum as article K8538.[20]

The following representation, which is suspected of being a copy of the original, is of the Sumerian clay tablet, with eight divisions for the eight constellations visible in the night sky. The other four were not visible. This provides evidence that the twelve main constellations were known before 3100 BC.

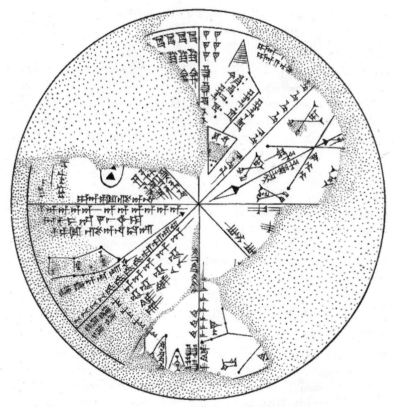

Fig. 8 Assyrian Planisphere – K8538. The British Museum, London. From: The British Museum. January 18, 2016.

Throughout the history of astronomy, people once thought the earth stood still, and the sun, moon, and stars rotated around it. Even today, we continue to say the sun rises and sets, when in reality, the sun does not move.

When man first looked up into the night sky, he saw the beauty and splendor of God's handiwork. As the night progressed, he noticed that some stars moved toward the west, and new groups of stars rose in the east. Stars toward the north moved very little, if at all. From that moment forward, man would look up at the stars and watch a very slow moving picture show. Over time, the creative imagination developed images and stories to go with the nightly scene.

Becoming more observant, man began to understand the seasons; summer and winter (or spring, summer, winter, and fall) came and went when certain constellations were visible, or when they appeared or disappeared. The more astute inscribed these images on cave walls, scrolls, clay tablets, or stone. In some civilizations, these astronomers were regarded very highly, and some were called priests. These priests could predict when the seasons would change; for example, in Egypt, they knew when the Nile River would flood.

What is astonishing is that throughout the different civilizations, separated by many miles of land and sea, many people identified some of the same grouping of stars and interpreted nearly the same image of the star patterns. They also identified the order in which the constellations appeared. Most of the naming of the constellations we attribute to the ancient Greeks, but we have evidence man knew of their patterns long before the Greeks.

As astronomy progressed, we learned that the twelve constellations are stationed along Earth's elliptic. Today we identify these constellations with the zodiac. The following table shows the constellations, their common pattern used today, and the best viewing time for each. After the table, I will review four key constellations.[21]

	Constellation (Latin)	Constellation (Hebrew)	Today's Common Pattern	Best Viewed
1.	Taurus	Shor	The Bull	January
2.	Gemini	Te'omim	The Twins	February
3.	Cancer	Sartan	The Crab	March
4.	Leo	Aryeh	The Lion	April
5.	Virgo	Betulah	The Virgin	May
6.	Libra	Moznayim	The Weigh Scales	June
7.	Scorpius	'Akrab	The Scorpion	July
	Ophiuchus	Afeichus	Serpent-Bearer	July

8.	Sagittarius	Keshet	The Archer, or Teapot	August
9.	Capricornus	Gedi	The Goat Fish	September
10.	Aquarius	Deli	Man Pouring Water	October
11.	Pisces	Dagim	Two Fish	November
12.	Aires	Taleh	The Ram	December

Taurus, Latin for "Bull"

Taurus was one of the first constellations I learned to identify in the night sky. At the start of this study, Taurus was the constellation appearing in the eastern sky near Orion, which I tracked each night until it disappeared behind the treetops as summer neared.

I have shown this constellation to strangers and provided a biblical background for this grouping of stars. Best seen in January, Taurus has been identified by many as a bull. Some draw the head of a bull with really long horns, while others draw out a full body.

One fascinating star is the left eye of the bull, a reddish-orange twinkling star called Aldebaran. This star has been measured to be forty-four times larger than our sun. If placed in the position of our sun, the edges of Aldebaran would occupy half the distance to the planet Mercury.

In Ancient Persia, Aldebaran[22] was identified as one of the Four Royal Stars, the other three being Regulus in Leo; Antares, found in Scorpio; and Fomalhaut, near Aquarius.

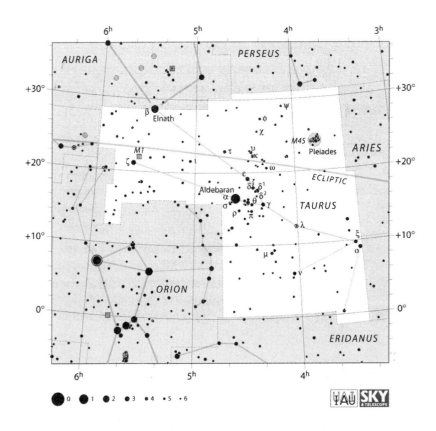

Patterns Recognized by Different Civilizations

Civilization	Pattern
Sumerians	Bull of the Milky Way
Greek	Bull
Hebrew	The Bull
Arabic	The Bull
Egyptian	The Apis Bull
Babylonian	The Bull of Heaven
Chinese	Golden Bull
Sanskrit	A Bull

The Leo Constellation

As the winter progressed and spring was nearing, I caught my first glimpse of Leo late one night in March. I underestimated how huge this constellation appears in the night sky in spring. At this point in my nascent astronomy interest, I had identified smaller constellations—the Pleiades, Aries, and Taurus—and a rather large one, Orion.

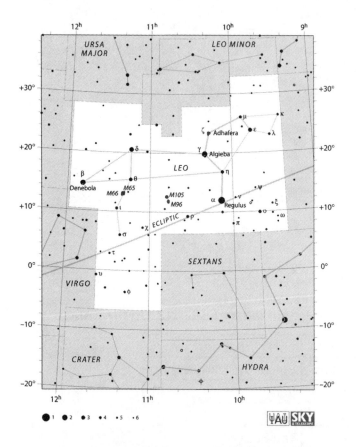

The first time Leo came into full view, I was impressed with the amount of night sky covered by this constellation. I actually went inside the house and pulled my wife outside to show her the beauty and magnificence of the lion in the sky.

Best seen in April, the Leo constellation is one that actually looks exactly its pattern: a lion. Regulus, one of the Royal Stars of the Babylonians, is in the front leg, or paw.

Patterns Recognized by Different Civilizations

Civilization	Pattern
Greek	Lion
Hebrew	The Lion
Arabic	The Lion
Egyptian	Lion, Sphinx
Babylonian	Lion
Chinese	Golden Lion
Sanscrit	A Lion
Mayan	A Frog*

*Frog (Lions are not indigenous to Mexico.)

Scorpius and Ophiuchus

Best seen in July, Scorpius is one of the brightest constellations in the night sky, yet in the early mornings of April, this constellation can be seen in all its wonder and beauty. Having waited a few months to see this constellation, I had a reaction similar to the first time I saw Leo. The time was 5 a.m., and pulling my wife out bed to show her would not have been a good idea. I quietly went inside the house and grabbed my tripod and camera. I was in awe of how this constellation towered over the neighborhood.

This constellation was the first key to unlocking the biblical identifications of the thirteen constellations around the elliptic in the Bible, and I had waited several months to see it. When reading the verse in the Bible where this pattern is found, I was also displaying the Scorpius constellation on my computer screen. At that moment, I realized the patterns of the constellations had been described in the Bible by Jacob in Genesis 49. Later on, I realized Ophiuchus was also included in the Bible, in the same verse where I found the pattern of Scorpius.

This will become more meaningful in the second section of the book, yet it depends on how one connects the dots and interprets the image in the night sky. In ancient biblical text, I will show how this constellation has two different patterns.

The Royal Babylonian Star Antares, toward the center of the defined constellation boundaries, is seven hundred times the size of the sun. In fact, it would encompass the planet of Mars if centrally placed in the location of our sun.

The constellation of Ophiuchus is located above Scorpius, and astronomers consider it as one of the constellations on the elliptic, except it is not part of the zodiac. At first, I was not interested in Ophiuchus. Then I realized the text in the Bible used to describe Scorpius also included Ophiuchus.

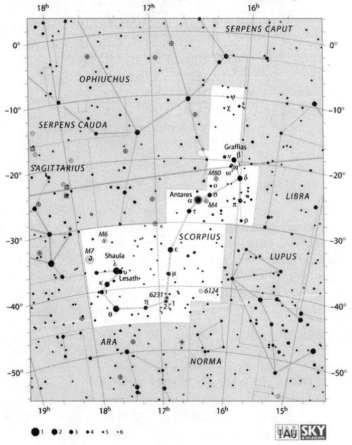

Patterns Recognized by Different Civilizations

Civilization	Scorpius Pattern	Ophiuchus Pattern
Greek	A Scorpion	Serpent Holder
Hebrew	The Scorpion	The Serpent Held
Arabic	The Scorpion	The Serpent Held
Egyptian	Scorpion / Serpent	Serpent Holder, Imhotep
Babylonian	Scorpion	Serpent Holder

Aquarius

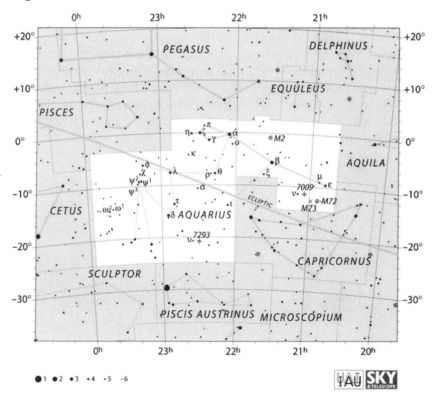

Located in the water or sea section of the night sky, Aquarius is the tenth largest constellation and the least illuminated. Most civilizations called this a water urn or vase, yet the IAU traced a man pouring out water from a vase. Due to its faintness, I have had difficulties seeing all the stars with the naked eye.

Patterns Recognized by Different Civilizations

Civilization	Pattern
Greek	Water Flowing
Hebrew	Water Urn
Arabic	Water Urn
Egyptian	Water Carrier
Babylonian	Great One with Over-flowing Vases
Chinese	Precious Vase
Sanscrit	Water Vase

Now that the twelve (or rather, thirteen) constellations of the zodiac have been identified, the question was, *How did the ancients use them to know the seasons?* The next step was to draw a model with the earth orbiting the sun with the twelve constellations in the backdrop, which creates the appearance of a clock. Although the sun does not move, some use the perspective from Earth to say, the sun in a specific constellation, therefore identifying the season.

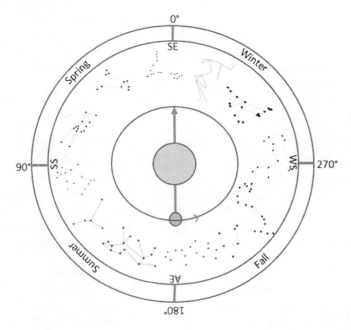

I drew the model above in an effort to best approximate the location and size of the constellations. The astronomical calendar 2015 and star mapping software provided the coordinates where the sun first touches the established boundaries of the constellations. The spring equinox is in the 0° location of the circle, the same location as defined by astronomers. If you recall, the Sumerians used the Atlas star of the Pleiades as their starting point, which is located on the back of Taurus.

As Earth rotates around the sun, the position of the sun from Earth's viewpoint points to a constellation, which can be referenced to a season.

Having an engineering background, I tend to comprehend processes and complex problems best when I have a model. I found this concept also works well for the Bible. Models are very useful tools, providing visual imagery over the sole use of grammatical text to illustrate what is being described. (In the second section of the book, I'll show how drawing out a model showed me an awesome symbolism I would have never considered.)

How does the model of the twelve constellations assist in the relationship of the Mazzaroth and the seasons? Looking back at the verse where the word is found, God may be asking if Job can speed up the rotation of the stars around Earth's elliptic, bringing forth the *seasons* sooner.

An interesting topic we will review later demonstrates how, over a long period of time, the seasons do not always line up with the same constellations. Four thousand years ago, for example, springtime would start in the constellation of Taurus instead of Pisces, as it does today. This seasonal shift in the constellations is due to the influence of gravitational forces from the sun and the moon on Earth as it orbits the sun, called the precession of the axis. Reviewing this effect later may favor a different meaning for the word "Mazzaroth."

The following sections will deal with the science of astronomy, which is necessary for understanding yet another facet of the Mazzaroth. I am going to explain a little how the earth's rotation and orbit works so we can have a better understanding of the stars and see God's amazing workmanship. I know this next part may be difficult for some, yet I did not have a full grasp until I studied it. At the end of each section, I have made a statement in bold for the main points to take away in my search for the meaning of the Mazzaroth.

The Earth and Sun Relationship

"The Earth was small, light blue, and so touchingly alone, our home that must be defended like a holy relic. The Earth was absolutely round. I believe I never knew what the word round meant until I saw Earth from space."[23]

—Aleksei Leonov, USSR

Earth, the third planet from the sun, has a round, spherical-like shape, which is tilted by approximately 23.5°. This recline in the earth is important to note and remember, for this gives us the seasons and changes the amount of daylight we experience over the course of a year.

The following illustration shows the tilt of the earth, the equator, and its rotation.

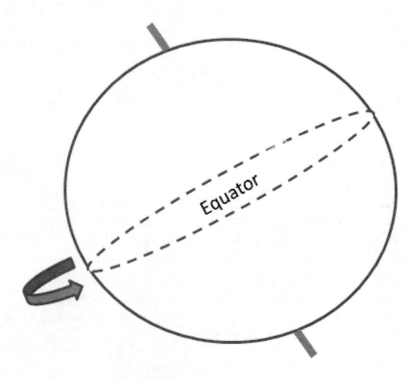

The circumference around the center of Earth, which is the widest, is called the equator. Earth spins from west to east at a speed of 1,040 miles

per hour (1,675 km/h) and rotates a distance of 24,902 miles (40,075 km), measured at the equator. I always knew the concept of rotation, but I did not understand the effect until one night I was facing east, watching the stars rise over the horizon. I imagined being at the top of a roller coaster, knowing I was heading down, but unable to see what was below.

An interesting tidbit about the rotation of the earth—the further one goes away from the equator, north or south, the slower the rotation, and at the poles, the rotation of Earth is so slow, it appears to barely rotate.

Earth is not perfectly spherical, for the meridional circumference, measured north to south, is 24,860 miles (40,008 km), making the earth bulge out slightly in the east to west direction. The slight bulge in the earth will cause us to experience another effect seen later.

There is a purpose for the tilt of the earth and the slight bulge as Earth rotates. This was a part of God's design for the earth to have seasons, and for the precession of the axis.

Measuring the rotation of the earth and relating to our concept of a day can be tricky, depending on your perspective. Looking from outer space at the North or South Pole, the earth completes one rotation in twenty-three hours and fifty-six minutes, called a sidereal day; however, it takes exactly twenty-four hours, or a solar day, for the sun to return to exactly the same spot in the sky.

At first I thought the solar day confirmed the Genesis passage for using stars to measure a day. Astronomers considered the sun to be a star and used it to measure a complete day; however, in the Bible, the sun is never referenced as a star. For the ancient Hebrews, the day began when the first star was visible in the late evening sky, and the daylight hours began when the bright morning star, the last star shining in the early morning, disappeared.

As we journey through the science of astronomy, I hope you have a better appreciation and awareness of the biblical implication of our review. When reading the creation story of the evening and the morning as the first day, I now have a better grasp of the cutoff times from day to day and how this knowledge can be used to further understand the biblical timing of events that happened throughout the day.

Continuing on with the movements of Earth, as the earth is spinning, it is also orbiting the sun at a rate of 18.5 miles per second (30 km/s), at 67,000 miles per hour (108,000 km/h). On its journey around the sun, the earth travels 584 million miles (939,856,896 km) completing one orbit. On average the earth is 92.96 million miles (149.605 million km) away from the sun.

The sun is 109 times the size of Earth, making the distance around the equator of the sun 2,713,406 miles (4,366,813 km), compared to Earth's 24,902 miles (40,075 km). Hypothetically, it would take a passenger airplane six months to orbit the sun.

The following illustration represents the earth's orbit around the sun. To be to scale, the size of the orbit needs to be tripled. From the toy solar system models I saw in elementary school, I did not realize how small Earth is compared to the sun, nor did I know Arcturus is 25 times; Aldebaran, 44 times; and Canis Majoris, 1,800 times the size of our sun!

I began to reflect on how miniscule the size of the earth is to the sun in comparison with other planets . . . and how insignificant our solar system is in the universe.

The immensity of the universe, the earth a mere nothing, and I, I am less. Yet the Creator observes and cares for us all, being mindful of an undeserving ingrate such as I. As there is no measure to an ever- expanding universe, given the depths of His love have no magnitude, how can one come to a full appreciation of His magnificence and omnipotence?

After reflecting on the miniscule size of our planet, I next considered that the average distance of the earth to the sun is not equal at all points around the orbit. The course of the earth is not a perfect circle, but elliptical in shape and slightly off center, having a maximum and minimum distance to the sun.

The point where the earth is closest to the sun is called the perihelion; conversely, the aphelion is where the earth is farthest from the sun. In the summer and winter months, the earth is at its closest and farthest point from the sun by about 1.8 million miles.

Table of the Earth's Distance from the Sun

Mean Distance	92,956,050 miles	149,598,262 km
Mean Aphelion	94,509,460 miles	152,098,233 km
Mean Perihelion	91,402,640 miles	147,098,291 km

Here is a trick question to consider. Which season would the earth be in when it is at the perihelion point, closest to the sun? The answer might surprise you. It depends on which side of the equator you are on.

The summer and winter seasons are not influenced by proximity to the sun, but by the amount of light exposure due to the tilt of the earth. The longest day of the year of the Northern Hemisphere is called the summer solstice, which begins the summer season. The shortest day is called the winter solstice and is officially the beginning of winter in the Northern Hemisphere. For the Southern Hemisphere the seasons are reversed.

Two days of the year mark the beginning of springtime and the beginning of the fall season. These two days are called the equinoxes, where there are approximately equal amounts of daylight and nighttime, but the exact day depends on your location on the planet.

There are a few lessons and applications to be learned from this odd occurrence of exposure versus proximity. Here is one that came to mind: Christianity is not only how close we are to God but also the amount of "light" exposure we emanate to others.

The main point to take away from this section is that there are four days of the year that mark the beginning of the seasons, which are based on the position of the earth from the sun.

The following diagram is a non-scalar representation of the four seasons grouped by Northern and Southern hemispheres. Notice the tilt of the earth's axis with relationship to the sun and the amount of light exposure, influencing the seasons.

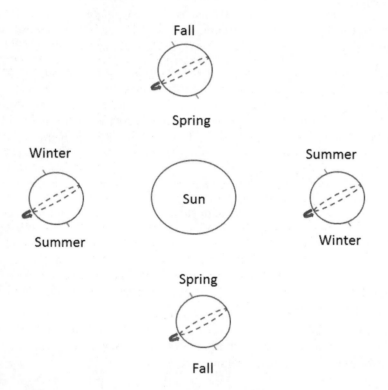

Measuring a Year

Did you know there are different methods for measuring a year? They can be very complex and hands-on to determine. First, we will explore methods using the earth's relationship to the sun and stars. Second, we'll review how the moon was and is used to measure a year. The importance is to understand how years are measured scientifically, and how a year is measured in the Bible. Here is a hint: they are not the same.

Most civilizations use a method called the solar year, which measures the amount of time to travel between the two equinoxes, or the same position in the cycle of seasons. The equinoxes are the two days in the year when the tilt of the earth and position to the sun provide equal amounts of daytime and nighttime, and are referred to as the spring and autumn equinox.

This measurement yields the year to be 365 days, 5 hours, 48 minutes, and 46 seconds, but in short we call it 365 ¼ days. The quarter day is where the Gregorian calendar adds an extra day to February every four years, called a leap year.[24]

Equivalent to a solar year, a tropical year is derived from the summer and winter solstices, where the sun reaches the highest point in the sky at 23.5° north of the equator, called the Tropic of Cancer, and the lowest point in the sky at 23.5° south of the equator, called the Tropic of Capricorn. Remember the angle of the tilt of the earth?

The measurement yields the year to be equal to that of the solar year. When these tropical lines were named approximately two thousand years ago, the summer and winter solstices were in the constellations Capricorn and Cancer. We'll review this further in the section regarding Earth's relationship to the stars. The spring and autumn equinoxes arrive when the sun's location is at the equator.

The following illustration shows the location of the sun with respect to the earth's tilt and location in its orbit. When the sun reaches the highest point in the Tropic of Cancer, it is summer in the Northern Hemisphere; when reaching the lowest point, it is summer in the Southern Hemisphere. The sun's location at the equator marks the equinoxes, where there are equal amounts of day and night.

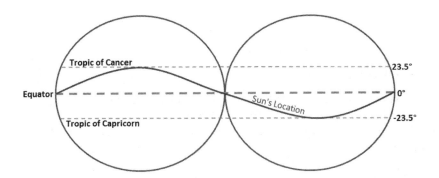

The previous illustration also explains how the Arctic Circle and Antarctica do not receive sunlight during their winter months. When the sun is in the Tropic of Cancer, Antarctica is totally dark; likewise, when the sun is in the Tropic of Capricorn, the Arctic Circle is dark.

Another way of viewing the solstices and equinoxes is to gauge the position of the sun in the sky with respect to the horizon. The following illustration, with the two solstices and equinoxes, shows the location of the sun in the sky as the earth rotates.

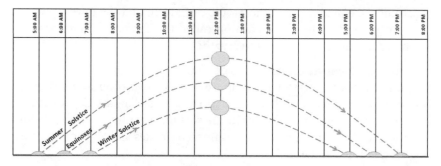

Throughout history, mankind has tried to determine and mark the position of these three points in the daytime sky to come up with an accurate measurement for the year. The position of the sun in our sky is another way of determining the seasons.

The Earth and Stars Relationship — Precession of the Axis

Another method to determine a year, called a sidereal year, measures the amount of time the earth orbits with respect to a fixed star. Basically, one could align with a star in the night sky, fix this location, and measure how much time passes until the selected star is in the exact location. I imagine this is the method Moses used in the wilderness.

Using this approach measures the orbit of the earth to the fixed stars at 20 minutes and 24.5 seconds longer than the average solar year. Twenty minutes does not seem like a lot, especially with respect to the earth traveling 584 million miles to complete one orbit; however, over a long period of time, those twenty minutes add up and significantly shift the stars from the equinoxes. This is the effect of the precession of the axis.

The precession of the axis, accredited to Hipparchus, a Greek astronomer between 200 and 100 BC, is probably one of the more difficult concepts of the movements of the earth to understand, so it may be best explained by illustrations.

When first describing the shape of the earth, I mentioned it is not perfectly spherical; it actually bulges *out* near the equator. As the earth is spinning, this imperfection causes the earth to slowly wobble like a top, creating a circular-like revolution of the axis. Over a period of 25,772 years, this wobble completes one revolution.[25]

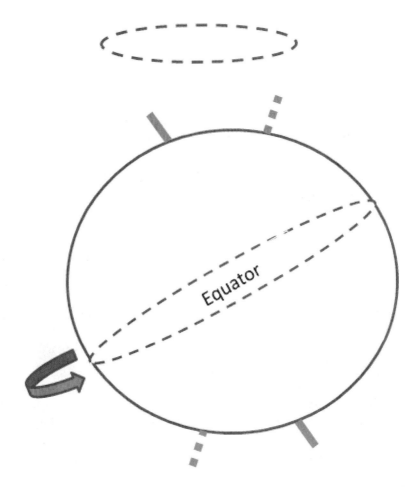

After creating the illustration of the precession of the axis, I took notice of the circle the axis makes above the earth. Later on I saw the following verse in Isaiah:

> "He sits enthroned above the circle of the earth, and its people are like grasshoppers. He stretches out the heavens like a canopy, and spreads them out like a tent to live in."
>
> —Isaiah 40:22 KJV

Did Isaiah understand the precession of the axis by calling it a circle above the earth? This would mean the ancients, at least by the eighth century BC, understood the precession of the axis before the Greeks. Historians also have clues the ancients knew of the effect of the precession long before the Greeks.

Being focused on astronomy, I noticed something else in this verse: the heavens being stretched out. Is it possible Isaiah, who lived between the eighth and seventh century BC, understood the expansion of the universe and the rotation of the earth? Five times he mentions the heavens being stretched out. Ponder the following verses: Isaiah 40:22, 42:5, 44:24, 45:12, and 51:13.

> "I have made the earth, and created man upon it: I, even my hands, have stretched out the heavens, and all their host have I commanded."
>
> —Isaiah 45:12

The Hubble telescope provided a means for looking farther out into the universe, but we have come to realize the more we look to understand and grasp the universe, the faster it expands.

The result of earth's wobble causes the alignment to the stars and constellations to shift with respect to the spring equinox. Not only will the constellations shift, but the current North Star, Polaris, will not be aligned with Earth's North Pole in the distant future. Five thousand years ago, the North Pole was pointed at a star called Thuban.

When archaeologists study ancient landmarks, they have to recall the effects of the precession of the axis to determine if the structures were aligned to the stars, sun, moon, or something else. This also helps in dating the site.

Axial precession has also interfered with ancients who identified markers in the sky. The four Royal Stars of the ancient Babylonians,[26] located in Taurus (N), Leo (W), Scorpio (S), and Aquarius (E), were considered guardians of the north, south, east, and west. This worked for a few centuries until the precession caused the equinox to drift and the cardinal points no longer lined up with their guardians.

For a constellation along the elliptical to shift 1° from the distance of the spring equinox takes 71.5889 years, and to drift 30° into another constellation, depending on the size and defined boundaries of the constellation, takes 2,150 years. Using the stars to determine the season works well over a few lifetimes, but over long time spans, this methodology will not be accurate. Does this put a flaw in our assessment that the Mazzaroth is seasonally based?

The earth's slow wobble over a long period of time prevents using the stars as a true measurement for the seasons.

In our 2015 star model of the twelve constellations, the spring equinox is near the far right side of the constellation Pisces. Due to the effects of axial precession approximately 2,100 years before, the spring equinox was just exiting the last star of the constellation Aries, which I considered to be the nose of the ram.

Herein lies a major difference between astronomy and astrology. Astrology is based on the **sign of Aries** starting in the 0° location and having a size of 30° of the earth's orbital rotation. Since this does not match with the actual constellation, the 30° portion is called the **sign of Aries**.

Astronomers use the exact position and size of the constellations with respect to the current location of the spring equinox. Most people know their astrological sign, but it may not be the actual constellation the sun was located when they were born.

Although my intent was to keep astrology out of this book, I felt it necessary to visually demonstrate the differences between astronomy and

astrology, giving you the ability to distinguish between the two and make your own decision with regard to astrology. Please refer to the following illustration.[27]

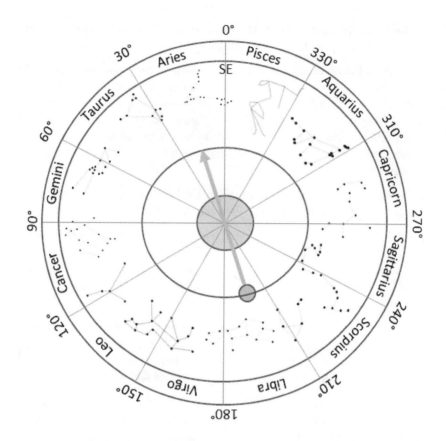

At the top of the outer circle is a marker of 0°. Astronomers place the spring equinox, designated with SE, at the 0° mark, yet astrologers place the beginning of the **sign of Aries** at the 0° mark and extend the size of the **sign of Aries** 30°. Each astrological sign is given 30°, completing the circle (12 x 30° = 360°).

The outer portion of the circle labels the degrees right to left, the same as the orbit of the earth. The next section is the naming of the sign of each 30° section. The connected dots, which form the common pattern for the constellation, are in the current position in the sky along with their size, which I attempted to draw to scale with respect to the spring equinox.

For the 2015 year, the constellation of Aries is physically located at 29.03° and occupies 24.4° of space within the circle.

As you see in the illustration, the sign of Aries contains the majority of the Pisces constellation, occupying 30° of space within the circle of Earth's orbit. This shows the difference between astronomers and astrologers with regard to their use of the zodiac. The development of the zodiac divided the orbit of Earth into twelve equal sections and applied the sign of the constellation to the section, with the 0° marker beginning with Aries. At the time of the zodiac's development, the constellation Aries was near the 0° marker, but there was no method of adjustment for the precession of the axis. The precession of the axis strikes again!

A different way to visually demonstrate the effects of axial precession is to model the spring equinox's changing position over time with respect to the backdrop of the twelve constellations. Considering the complexities involved in astrophysics, calculating the position of the equinox over time is elementary.

The astronomical calendar 2015 or star mapping software provides the positions of the constellations in degrees from the spring equinox. On April 19, 2015, the sun entered the constellation Aries at the 29.03° mark. This means the first defined astronomical point of Aries is located 29.03° from the spring equinox in 2015. One degree of precession is approximately equal to 71.589 years, and we multiply the number of years by the degrees from the spring equinox to arrive at the year the spring equinox was at the nose of the lamb in Aries:

29.03° x 71.589 years/degree is approximately 2,078 years ago

2,015 AD – 2,078 = –63 BC

One astronomy resource, Earthsky.org, calculated that the last time the spring equinox was in Aires was in 68 BC.[28] From an amateur astronomer's perspective, I am pretty close, yet our boundary for Aires and calculation for the precession may be slightly different. Here is the model showing the precession of the spring and autumn equinox at four points in time.

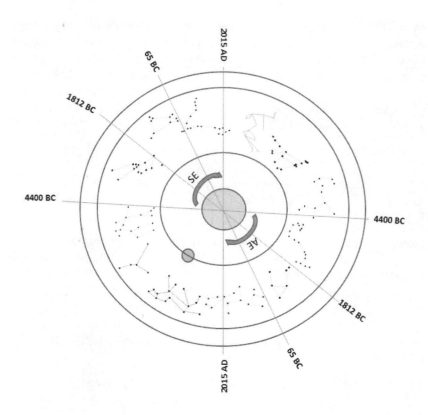

Calculating the position of the spring and autumn equinox over time gives us the time periods the spring equinox was "inside" a constellation.

Hopefully, you have survived this section and have a better grasp on the precession of the axis and the effects on the position of the equinoxes. At the conclusion of this book, we will revisit this model, applying dates and biblical significance to the constellations, but, for now, let's finish up the astronomy session.

The Moon

Science teaches us that the moon, visually the largest object in the night sky, is comparably small when compared to the actual size of the stars and planets. Although small in actual size, biblically the moon has several important roles.

While the earth is spinning on its axis and orbiting the sun, the moon is also spinning and orbiting the earth, tagging along with the earth around the sun. The orbit of the moon around earth is called the celestial equator.

The moon is considerably small, with a circumferential distance of 2,159 miles (3,474 km) around its equator, and travels 2,288 miles per hour (3,683 km/h) around the earth. The average distance from the earth to the moon is 238,900 miles (384,400 km), taking 27.322 days to rotate around its axis and 27.322 days to orbit around the earth.

Did you catch the last sentence? The elapsed time for the moon to rotate once on its axis is *equal* to its revolution around the earth. The rotation of the moon on its axis is slow due to an effect astronomers call tidal lock, which slows the rotation of a small body until it is synchronized with its period of revolution around the larger body.[29] Most of the moons in our solar system display this effect. The amount of time for the rotation and orbit of the moon is amazingly equal.

This effect, also called synchronous rotation, allows us to see only one side of the moon from Earth. The other side of the moon is never seen, which is why many people have labeled it the "dark side of the moon." This strange rotation and orbital combination provides the phases or cycles of the moon, which is based on the reflection of the sun's light and position of the moon with respect to Earth. The phases of the moon take 29 days, 12 hours, and 44 minutes to complete, for the moon takes an extra 2.2 days to catch up with the earth's orbit around the sun.

Based on the position of the moon with respect to the sun and earth, we observe a full moon; a dark moon, called a new moon; and a variety of phases of the moon, as a non-scalar illustration shows.

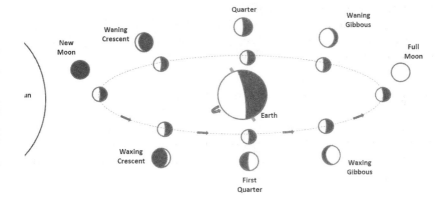

As mentioned earlier, some civilizations, including today's, have a lunar-based calendar system founded on the phases of the moon, and the new moon marks the beginning for each month. Using a lunar-based calendar system calculates the number of days in a year to 354 days. Today, lunar calendar systems are still used by Arabic nations, and no adjustments are made with respect to the sun.

Other civilizations, both today and in the ancient world, used the new moon to mark the beginning of the month, but days or an extra month were added to line up with the equinoxes or solar year. This type of calendar system is called a Lunar-Solar calendar and continues to be used by the Hebrews, the Chinese, and others.

Perigee and Apogee Moon

Similar to Earth's rotation around the sun, the moon's orbit around the earth is elliptical, having a point closest to the earth, called the perigee, and a point furthest from the earth, called an apogee. For this reason, some full moons appear larger than normal, due to the proximity of the moon to earth. In rare occasions, the moon gets very close to the earth and appears really large. NASA calls this a super perigee moon.

According to NASA, the last super perigee moon was on March 19, 2011; before that, it was seen in March 1993. The next one is calculated to appear on November 25, 2034. In general, perigee moons are 14 percent larger and 30 percent brighter than the moon normally appears.

Halo around the Moon

An interesting observance of the moon is called a halo around the moon, which some call a ring around the moon. This event does not happen every night, but does happen rather frequently. The halo occurs when tiny ice crystals from high cirrostratus clouds are formed, refracting light at 22°.

During the day, a similar halo can be seen around the sun, and if one looks close enough at the ring (but remember: looking directly at the sun can be damaging to your eyes), the ring has the colors of a rainbow.

NASA claims they are not sure exactly how the ice crystals form in the clouds, but it is an amazing part of creation to enjoy.

Solar and Lunar Eclipses

The last phenomenon of the sun, earth, and moon to discuss is eclipses. There are two types of eclipses: a solar eclipse occurs when a new moon passes in front of the sun, casting a shadow on Earth, and a lunar eclipse occurs when the earth passes in front of the sun, casting a shadow on the moon in the full phase.

As the moon orbits Earth, its angle of trajectory changes with each orbit. Without this angular change, we would have a solar eclipse with every new moon, or conversely, we would never have a solar eclipse.

A solar eclipse is an eerie experience, for there is darkness similar to night-time when daylight should be present. Safely observing a total solar eclipse, one will see the moon perfectly covers the sun. Consider the implications of the moon perfectly covering the sun as you review the four types of solar eclipses.

Partial eclipse. The angle of the moon's orbit does not fully encompass the sun.

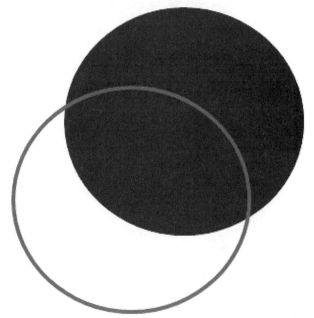

Annular eclipse. The moon's distance from the earth is farther, so it appears smaller and almost blocks out the sun, leaving a ring of fire. Remember the visual size of the moon when it is in apogee, farther away from the earth?

Total eclipse. The moon's distance from the earth and the angle of its orbit perfectly blocks out the sun.

Hybrid eclipse. This type of eclipse shifts from a total and an annular eclipse depending on which point on the earth's surface one is viewing.

Viewing a total solar eclipse from outer space would appear like the following sketch. The moon's shadow on earth is approximately 4,000 miles (8,800 km) in diameter.

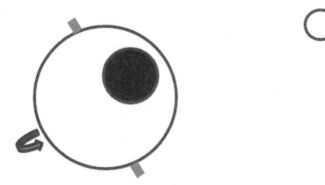

Consider the setup for a total solar eclipse. First, the changing orbital angle of the moon around the earth must be in alignment with the sun, and is in the phase of a new moon. The distance from the earth and distance of the earth from the sun places the moon so that the sun is perfectly blocked out. The sun is 1,262 times the size of the moon! In the event where the moon is a little farther from the earth, remember apogee: the moon will appear to have a ring of fire around the edges.

Some believe the creation of the universe was a random event. The stars, planets and suns, and other celestial bodies randomly fell into their locations, yet the position of the earth, sun, and moon perfectly align during a total solar eclipse. Those who believe this was a random event have more faith than I do, for I can only conclude this shows God was involved in creation. The sizes, speeds, angles, and distances were not accidental nor coincidental.

In the future, the angles of orbital rotation of the moon will change to where a total solar eclipse will no longer occur.

The second type of eclipse, the lunar eclipse, occurs when the earth comes between the moon and the sun. Like the solar eclipse, the same four types of eclipses can occur. During a total lunar eclipse, the moon will turn a dark reddish color and the earth, from the moon's perspective, will have a ring of fire around the edges.

NASA provides a searchable database with the history of solar and lunar eclipses.[30] One that caught my attention was the solar eclipse on March 19, 33 AD. The time of this solar eclipse was between the sixth and ninth hour, as cited in the four Gospels during the crucifixion, and lined up with the country of Israel.

Can we prove or disprove a solar eclipse occurred on the crucifixion day, allowing us to date the crucifixion? In constructing the ancient Hebrew calendar, this question will be reviewed and answered.

Ancient Hebrew Calendar

Let's conduct a scope check, and ask the question, "How does an ancient Hebrew calendar apply to the Mazzaroth?" The word "season" used in Job 38:32 can also emphasize the time of an event, like a festival, and constructing the ancient Hebrew calendar will show where specific events, called feasts, were placed.

Now that we have adventured through astronomy, learning some of the ordinances of the heavens, we have a better understanding of the movements of the earth, the moon, and their relationships to the stars. This will give a foundation for reconstructing an ancient Hebrew calendar God gave to Moses.

The ancient Hebrew calendar will provide insight and importance of their holidays and will enlighten us to the symbolism God reveals in the calendar. My first notion was to construct the calendar to aid in determining the number of days in the ancient Hebrew year; however, when I added the holidays and astronomical events, the symbolism jumped out from the pages. Can an ancient Hebrew calendar point to Christ and the end of days, adding to our evidence God knew the beginning from the end?

When is the last time you looked at a current Hebrew calendar? What day, month, and year is the nation of Israel using today? At the writing of this paragraph, the Gregorian date is June, 18, 2015, and the Hebrew date is 1 Tamuz, 5775. Are they using a different calendar than most civilizations do? Where did this come from, and why is the year 5775?

Please note the fundamentals of the Hebrew calendar have changed at least three times: the period after the exodus, during the Babylonian captivity, and in the current Hebrew calendar known today (which dates back to 359 AD, when Hillel II broke with tradition and developed rules for calculating the calendar[31]).

The Hebrew calendar dates back to ancient history, was kept by the priest, and considered a guarded secret. If it was a secret, how are we going to build an ancient Hebrew calendar? Has there been archaeological evidence of these calendars? Actually, one such calendar was found, the Gezer calendar, discovered in 1908 by R.A.S. McAllister.[32] It is dated to the tenth century BC, citing an annual cycle of agricultural activities. Unfortunately, it was not an official calendar, and like most ancient artifacts, there are varying theories and opinions as to its authenticity.

Here is how the calendar read:

Two months of fruit picking

Two months of grain sowing

Two months of late sowing

One month of flax harvest

One month of barley harvest

One month of wheat harvest

Two months of vine pruning

One month picking and drying figs

Since the Gezer calendar dated to the tenth century BC, it still does not give us much information for the first ancient Hebrew calendar. What other sources could we pull from? Is it possible the calendar is listed in the Bible? Funny, I do not remember seeing a calendar in the indexes, but I believe that through reading and studying, we might find the calendar does exist . . . and was not so much of a guarded secret.

The Bible provides rules for the construction of the ancient Hebrew calendar. The first is the establishment of a monthly calendar. Fifteen days before the children of Israel take their flight out of exodus and the last plague comes upon Egypt, God establishes the first month of the year, Abib.

"This month [Chodesh] shall be unto you the beginning of months [Chodesh]: it
shall be the first month [Chodesh] of the year to you."

—Exodus 12:2 KJV

"This day came ye out in the month Abib."

—Exodus 13:4

In the Hebrew language, the word for month is *Chodesh*,[33] which is also interpreted "new moon." Esoterically, Chodesh tells us to pay close attention to the details, for it is a sense of completeness and a doorway to spiritual knowledge.[34] This provides evidence the months of the ancient Hebrew calendar will be lunar based, where the first day of each month begins on a new moon.

The use of a new moon to mark the start of a month was not new to the ancient civilizations. The Sumerians used the new moon to mark the start of their calendar;[35] other civilizations used a full moon or a different phase of the moon.

This marks the beginning of the use of months for the Israelites by the Hebrew word "Chodesh." In Genesis, this word gives insight as to the author and the approximate date when the first book of the Bible was written.

According to Strong's numbers, the word for the first month, "Abib," means fresh young barley ears, with the root word meaning tender. This provides a clue that the first month was associated with the barley harvest. This may keep the alignment of the ancient Hebrew calendar with the spring equinox; however, in the works of Josephus Flavis, dated around 68 AD, he makes the following comments:

"In the month . . . called Nisan [Abib], and is the beginning of our year, on the fourteenth day of the lunar month, when the sun is in Aries, (for in this month it was that we were delivered from bondage under the Egyptians)."[36]

The Bible also tells us when the first month will begin.

"[T]hou shalt sacrifice the passover at even, at the going down of the sun, at the **season** that thou camest forth out of Egypt."

—Deuteronomy 16:6 (emphasis and brackets mine)

Remember: the Hebrew word used for season is Mow'ed, the same word used in Genesis, when the stars are used for seasons. **Josephus' statement and the Bible provide a clue that the feast of the Passover occurred when the sun was in the Aries constellation.**

If Moses were to fixate upon a star to determine the year, the visible constellation opposite of Aries would be Virgo. This may provide another clue that the calendar was also sidereal based. Aligning the Passover with the constellation Aries would show the stars being used for years. This may have been the marker Moses used to determine when the month of Abib began, for there is no record of barley being planted during the forty years in the wilderness—only mana and quail were in their diet. They also took down and set up camp forty-two times, making planting and harvesting very difficult.

After the wilderness journey, the ancient Hebrew calendar, as the first month, Abib, suggests, may be based on the barley harvest. This would apply once the children of Israel had settled in the Promised Land.

The next part of the calendar groups the days into weeks. The days are not named, only called Day 1, Day 2, etc., except the seventh day is called the Sabbath, a day of holy convocation and rest.

"Six days thou shalt do thy work, and on the seventh day thou shalt rest"

—Exodus 23:12

"Six days shall work be done, but the seventh day is a **Sabbath** of solemn rest, a holy convocation. You shall do no work on it; it is the Sabbath of the Lord in all your dwellings."

—Leviticus 23:3 (emphasis mine)

The setup of the day is another aspect of our ancient calendar that will help to understand days in the Bible. I have found this difficult to grasp, but the beginning of the day is not the same as today. Our day begins at midnight; however, in the creation story, the new day begins in the evening. Traditionally, this happens as the first star presents itself in the night sky. The night ends when the last star fades as the first burst of the sun's rays over the horizon blind us from seeing the last star.

"And God called the light Day, and the darkness he called Night. And the evening and the morning were the first day."

—Genesis 1:5

Division of days are given in four time frames: evening, night, morning and noon. In the Old Testament, the word "hour" is only found in the book of Daniel; however, hours were used in ancient Israel, for Isaiah mentions the sun dial of former King Ahaz.

Starting the construction of the calendar, we have the following:

Month – Abib (Young Barley)

	Day 1	Day 2	Day 3	Day 4	Day 5	Day 6	Sabbath
Evening							
Morning							

The next step in constructing our ancient Hebrew calendar is to determine the days in a month and, afterwards, the number of months in a year. This part of the calendar is found in the story of the Great Flood, and with a little diligence, you will find there were 30 days in a month, twelve months in a year for a total of 360 days in a year. If one desires to do the math, the verses are included on how I arrived at this conclusion.

> "In the six hundredth year of Noah's life, in the **second month**, the **seventeenth day** of the month, the same day were all the fountains of the great deep broken up, and the windows of heaven were opened."
>
> —Genesis 7:11 (emphasis mine)

> "And the waters prevailed upon the earth **an hundred and fifty days**."
>
> —Genesis 7:24 (emphasis mine)

> "[A]fter the end of the **hundred and fifty days** the waters were abated.
>
> And the ark rested in the **seventh month**, on the **seventeenth day** of the month, upon the mountains of Ararat."
>
> —Genesis 8:3–4 (emphasis and brackets mine)

At this point in the story, we have a course of five months, with 150 days, yielding 30 days in a month. This applies for months two through six. The total amount of days for months one, seven, eight, and nine are not recorded in this passage. From month ten to the first day of the next year, the math comes out to 61 days, yielding 30 days in months ten, eleven and twelve.

> "[I]n the tenth month, on the first day of the month, were the tops of the mountains seen."
>
> —Genesis 8:5 (brackets mine)

> "at the end of forty days, that Noah opened the window of the ark . . ."
>
> —Genesis 8:6

At the end of 40 days, a raven is sent from the ark, then a dove, and the following phrase is given, which I interpret to mean 7 days passed between the first and second dove.

> "And he stayed yet other **seven** days . . ."
>
> —Genesis 8:10 (emphasis mine)

The time between the second and third dove remained constant:

> "And he stayed yet other **seven** days . . ."
>
> —Genesis 8:12 (emphasis mine)

> "In the six hundredth and first year, in the **first month**, the **first day** of the month, the waters were dried up from off the earth."
>
> —Genesis 8:13 (emphasis mine)

40 + 7 + 7 +7 = 61 days

> "And in the **second month**, on the **seven** and **twentieth** day of the month, was the earth dried."
>
> —Genesis 8:14 (emphasis mine)

Growing up, I had thought Noah was confined inside the Ark for 40 days and nights, but after researching the Great Flood in greater detail, I learned Noah was in the ark for 370 days. Can you imagine the discomfort, foul smell, and amount of food needed to supply a family of eight and a boat full of animals?

I assumed months one, seven, eight, and nine have 30 days, so the construction of the ancient Hebrew calendar will have twelve months and 360 days in the year. Scholars call this a prophetic year, but the concept for a calendar of 360 days with 30 days per month was used early on by the Sumerians and Egyptians.

There are also other pre-Babylonian era references where 30 days are used in a month. See Deuteronomy 34:8, 21:13 and Numbers 20:29. First Chronicles 27:1–15 in fact lists twelve months in a year.

For the calendar, the Bible provides days and months, yet the number of days of the year is not specifically given, so we'll assume 360 days in the year for now (as previously calculated in our assessment of the Great Flood).

The last thing to complete on our ancient Hebrew calendar is the addition of holidays, called feasts. The feast will be significant in showing God's message, adding even more evidence that God knew the end from the beginning.

Paul stressed the importance of the feast days when he writes to the Colossians. This gives us a clue the ancient Hebrew calendar will be prophetic:

> "Let no man therefore judge you in meat, or in drink, or in respect of a festival, or of the new moon, or of the Sabbath days. Which are a shadow of things to come."
>
> —2 Colossians 2:16–17 NKJV

To add the holidays or feast days to our calendar, the Bible gives very detailed instructions on where to place the days and the required sacrifices. The rules for the feast days are found in Exodus, Leviticus, Numbers, and Deuteronomy. One must be studious and read the establishment of the feast in all places, for in some cases, a little extra is added in each book.

There is a lesson to be learned here. In taking a single verse of Scripture to prove a point or come to a conclusion, one may miss all the extras and the bigger picture.

I attempted to summarize and condense the rules of the feast days as follows.

The Passover of the Lord

The first holiday given for our calendar is the Passover, which is in the month of Abib. Before the exodus, the children of Israel selected a lamb on the tenth day of the first month, which they inspected for blemishes and spots. The lamb stays with them, is killed on the evening of the thirteenth, and eaten on the fourteenth a few hours later. This meal is referred to as the "Seder meal." Remember, the Hebrew day begins when the sun is no longer present and the first star appears in the late evening sky.

> "In the **tenth** day of this month they shall take to them every man a lamb, according to the house of their fathers, a lamb for an house.
>
> Your lamb shall be without blemish, a **male** of the first year: ye shall take it out from the sheep, or from the goats. And ye shall keep it up until the **fourteenth day** of the same month: and the whole assembly of the congregation of Israel shall **kill it in the evening**."
>
> —Exodus 12:4–6 KJV (emphasis mine)

> "In one house shall it be eaten; thou shalt not carry forth ought of the flesh abroad out of the house; **neither** shall ye **break a bone** thereof."
>
> —Exodus 12:46 (emphasis mine)

> "And in the fourteenth day of the first month is the Passover of the Lord."
>
> —Numbers 28:16

Let's look back at Josephus' statement concerning the timing of Passover, "when the sun is in Aries."

Using calculations along with the star software program *RedShift* ,[37] I placed the date of the Passover in 68 AD on April 3. How did I perform this calculation? The spring equinox in 68 AD was on March 21, placing it in the constellation of Pisces.

In that same year, the sun's position to the backdrop of the stars moved into the Aries constellation between March 26 and April 14. Since the Hebrew months begin with a new moon, the new moon was calculated to fall on the March 21, marking the first day of Nisan, formerly called Abib. Thirteen days later is April 3. This is based on the current Gregorian calendar method.

Ready to look at the stars and constellation for significance and symbolism? Josephus tells us Passover is celebrated when the sun is in Aires, for this is when the Hebrews came out of Egypt.

What is the common pattern today of Aries? A ram. Even the ancient Sumerians, determined as being one of the earliest civilizations to emerge in the world, identified the Aries constellation on a clay tablet star map as a lamb in 3123 BC.

From my calculations and timeline, the spring equinox first entered the constellation of Aries, the lamb, *sixty years* before the exodus. As time progressed, the spring equinox slowly shifted into the Pisces constellation around 63 BC. Approximately one hundred years later, the Passover Lamb, Jesus, was crucified, and in 72 AD, the temple would be destroyed, marking an end to the sacrifices.

Can you sense the coincidence? Is the positioning of the spring equinox Divine, providing evidence God knew the end from the beginning by

placing the stars in the sky to signify the seasons? In this instance, there was a Passover season symbolized in the Aries constellation, which soon ended when the spring equinox transitioned out of the constellation identified as a lamb.

I am grappling with how four little visible stars could have so much significance. To take this a step further, I wonder if the region of the wise men, who searched for Jesus, were given instruction to start looking for a celestial event after the spring equinox moved out of Aries.

Finally, during their Babylonian captivity, the Hebrews changed their month from Abib to Nisan, which means "their flight," yet the ancient Babylonians called their first month, related to Aries, the "sacrifice of righteousness."[38]

During a Wednesday night Bible study, we were asked to pick a name for God that was personal to us. I chose Jehovah-Shammah, found in the last four words in the book of Ezekiel, "the Lord is here." After tying together the significance of the Aries constellation to the Passover, crucifixion, and the first month of the Hebrews and Babylonians, God appears to me as the God who is here, there, and *everywhere.*

Feast of Unleavened Bread

The Feast of Unleavened Bread and the Lord's Passover are collectively combined into a single celebration called the Passover. Understanding

the merging of these two feasts will aide in deciphering specific days in the four Gospels. (On a personal note, I spent four days banging my head against a wall trying to figure out which day Christ was crucified until my eyes were open to understand the Feast of Unleavened Bread is sometimes called the Passover Feast, and the Passover Seder meal is on a different day. To limit my confusion, I show the Passover meal on the fourteenth, as the Seder.

The Feast of Unleavened Bread last seven days, beginning on the fifteenth, and ending at evening time on the twenty-first.

"**Seven days** shall ye eat unleavened bread; even the first day ye shall put away leaven out of your houses: And in the **first** day there shall be an holy convocation, and in the **seventh** day there shall be an holy convocation to you; no manner of work shall be done in them, save that which every man must eat, that only may be done of you. In the first month, on the fourteenth day of the month at even, ye shall eat unleavened bread, until the **one and twentieth** day of the month at even."

—Exodus 12: 15–16, 18 (emphasis mine)

"Six days thou shalt eat unleavened bread: and on the **seventh** day, shall be a **solemn assembly** to the Lord thy God: thou shalt do no work therein."

—Deuteronomy 16:8 (emphasis mine)

Feast of Firstfruits

The Feast of Firstfruits begins on the first day after the normal Sabbath day following the day of the Passover. This would be the first day of the week after Passover. This feast also signals the beginning of the grain harvest, starting with barley. The first yield of the grain harvest is waved before the Lord, called a sheaf offering.

"He shall wave the sheaf before the Lord, to be accepted on your behalf; on the **day after the Sabbath** the priest shall wave it. And you shall offer on that day, when you wave the sheaf, a **male lamb** of the first year, without blemish . . ."

—Leviticus 23:11–12 (emphasis mine)

Feast of Weeks (Pentecost)

The Feast of Weeks is a calculated holiday, depending on when the first yield of the land (Firstfruits) are harvested. This provides a clue that the ancient Hebrew calendar will not only be lunar and sidereal based but also agricultural based.

> "You shall count seven weeks for yourself; begin to count the seven weeks from the time you begin to put the sickle to the grain [Qamah]."
>
> —Deuteronomy 16:9 NKJV (brackets mine)

This verse provides an indication that the calendar may be adjusted based on the readiness of the grain to be harvested after the fall planting. Traditionally, I have read, the priest would inspect the barley in the field, and if it wasn't ready for the day of Firstfruits, another month would be added to the calendar.

We now have two methods for adjusting the lunar calendar of 354 days to be closer to a solar year, using Aires (for sidereal) and the agricultural growth of the barley.

The Feast of Weeks is a calculation of seven weeks, starting on the Sabbath after the Feast of Firstfruits. On the fiftieth day a new grain offering is required.

> "And ye shall count unto you from the morrow after the sabbath, from the day that ye brought the sheaf of the wave offering; **seven sabbaths** shall be complete: Even unto the morrow after the seventh sabbath shall ye number **fifty days**; and ye shall offer a new grain offering unto the LORD."
>
> —Leviticus 23:15–16 KJV (emphasis mine)

Feast of Trumpets

The Feat of Trumpets is in the first day of the seventh month, a new moon, and is treated as a Sabbath.

> "Speak unto the children of Israel, saying, In the seventh month, in the first day of the month, shall ye have a sabbath, a memorial of blowing of trumpets, an holy convocation."
>
> —Leviticus 23:24

> "And in the seventh month, on the first day of the month, ye shall have an holy convocation; ye shall do no servile work: it is a day of blowing the trumpets unto you."
>
> —Numbers 29:1

Day of Atonement

The Day of Atonement is on the tenth day of the seventh month and is treated as a Sabbath with fasting. It is a day of cleansing; the Jubilee trumpet is to be sounded every fifty years, and trumpets shall sound throughout all the land.

"Also on the tenth day of this seventh month there shall be a day of atonement: it shall be an holy convocation unto you; and ye shall afflict your souls, and offer an offering made by fire unto the LORD. It shall be unto you a sabbath of rest, and ye shall afflict your souls: in the **ninth day** of the month **at even**, from **even unto even**, shall ye celebrate your sabbath."

—Leviticus 23:27, 32 (emphasis mine)

"And you shall count seven sabbaths of years for yourself, seven times seven years; and the time of the seven sabbaths of years shall be to you forty-nine years. Then you shall cause the **trumpet of the Jubilee** to sound on the tenth day of the seventh month; on the Day of Atonement you shall make the trumpet to sound throughout all your land. And you shall consecrate the fiftieth year, and proclaim liberty throughout all the land to all its inhabitants. It shall be a Jubilee for you; and each of you shall return to his possession, and each of you shall return to his family."

—Leviticus 25:8–10 (emphasis mine)

Feast of Tabernacles

The last feast given for the ancient Hebrew calendar is the Feast of Tabernacles, lasting seven days. Native Israelites are to dwell in booths during this feast. The feast begins on the fifteenth of the seventh month, which is or is close to a full moon. God calls this the end of the year harvest, the feast of ingathering.

"Also on the fifteenth day of the seventh month, when you have gathered in the fruit of the land, you shall keep the feast of the Lord for seven days; on the first day there shall be a sabbath-rest, and on the eighth day a sabbath-rest. And you shall take for yourselves on the first day the fruit of beautiful trees, branches of palm trees, the boughs of leafy trees, and willows of the brook; and you shall rejoice before the Lord your God for seven days. You shall keep it as a feast to the Lord for seven days in the year. It shall be a statute forever in your generations. You shall celebrate it in the seventh month. You shall dwell in booths for seven days. All who are native Israelites shall dwell in booths,"

—Leviticus 23:36–39

The following verse tells us when to increase the number of the year.

"And thou shalt observe the feast of weeks, of the firstfruit of wheat harvest, and the feast of ingathering at the year's end."

—Exodus 34:22

The sacrifices for the Feast of Tabernacles, I believe, provide significance and symbolism. Pay special attention to the total number of sacrifices. This will prove instructive when the calendar is completed.

Day	1	2	3	4	5	6	7	Total
Young bull	13	12	11	10	9	8	7	70
Ram	2	2	2	2	2	2	2	14
Lamb	7	7	7	7	7	7	7	49
Goat	1	1	1	1	1	1	1	7

	Total	140

Other Feasts and Special Days

For the feast of Passover, there is a provision given for those who are on a long journey or unclean.

"Speak unto the children of Israel, saying, If any man of you or of your posterity shall be unclean by reason of a dead body, or be in a journey afar off, yet he shall keep the Passover unto the LORD. The **fourteenth day** of the **second month** at even they shall keep it, and eat it with unleavened bread and bitter herbs. They shall leave none of it unto the morning, nor break any bone of it: according to all the ordinances of the Passover they shall keep it."

—Numbers 9: 10–12 (emphasis mine)

Constructing the Calendar

The number of days in a week, months in a year, and holidays have been defined; however, the number of weeks and days in a year is not clearly stated in the Bible. Three hundred and sixty days were calculated in the Great Flood, assuming the missing months contain 30 days. Backing this assumption, three and a half years in Revelation 11:3 contain 1,260 days, which is 360 days in a year + 180 days for a half year.

For our ancient calendar, a year will initially contain 360 days, yet when the children of Israel come into the Promised Land, the initial number of days in a year will be adjusted to 354. The following pages are the product of my

Month 1 (Abib / Nissan)

	Day 1	Day 2	Day 3	Day 4	Day 5	Day 6	Sabbath
						1 New Moon	2
	3	4	5	6	7	8	9
	10 Lamb Selected	11	12	13 Lamb Slain	14 Seder Meal	15 Full Moon Special Sabbath Passover Feast →	16
	17 Day 1 Firstfruits	18 Day 2	19 Day 3	20 Day 4	21 Special Sabbath Day 5 End of Passover	22 Day 6	23 Sabbath 1 Day 7
	24 Day 8	25 Day 9	26 Day 10	27 Day 11	28 Day 12	29 Day 13	30 Sabbath 2 Day 14

Month 2 (Ziv / Iyar)

	Day 1	Day 2	Day 3	Day 4	Day 5	Day 6	Sabbath
	1 New Moon Day 15	2 Day 16	3 Day 17	4 Day 18	5 Day 19	6 Day 20	7 Sabbath 3 Day 21
	8 Day 22	9 Day 23	10 Day 24	11 Day 25	12 Day 26	13 Day 27	14 Sabbath 4 Day 28 2nd Passover
	15 Full Moon Day 29	16 Day 30	17 Day 31	18 Day 32	19 Day 33	20 Day 34	21 Sabbath 5 Day 35
	22 Day 36	23 Day 37	24 Day 38	25 Day 39	26 Day 40	27 Day 41	28 Sabbath 6 Day 42
	29 Day 43	30 Day 44					

	Day 1	Day 2	Day 3	Day 4	Day 5	Day 6	Sabbath
Month 3 (??? / Sivan)			1 New Moon Day 45	2 Day 46	3 Day 47	4 Day 48	5 Sabbath 7 Day 49
	6 Day 50 Feast of Weeks	7	8	9	10	11	12
	13	14	15 Full Moon	16	17	18	19
	20	21	22	23	24	25	26
	27	28	29	30			

	Day 1	Day 2	Day 3	Day 4	Day 5	Day 6	Sabbath
Month 7 (Ethanim / Tishri)				1 New Moon Feast of Trumpets	2	3	4
	5	6	7	8	9	10 50th Year Jubilee Trumpet Day of Atonement	11
	12	13	14	15 Full Moon Special Sabbath Feast of Tabernacles	16	17	18
	19	20	21 End Feast of Tabernacles	22 Special Sabbath Solemn Assembly	23	24	25
	26	27	28	29	30		

research to construct the ancient Hebrew calendar. I only show months one through three, and month seven.

360 vs. 365 Days in a Year

Using the account of the Great Flood, I arrived at a year with 360 days, yet this puzzled me, for we have perfected the measurements to 365 ¼ days. I researched the calendars of the ancient Sumerians and Egyptians and found they also had twelve month per year, 30 days per month, and 360 days per year in their calendars.[39]

There was evidence 5 days per year were added at the end of their ancient calendars, and that they considered the extra days to be unlucky. It was unclear when the extra 5 days were added, but it is worth noting, that these civilizations originally had 360-day calendars as well. There seemed to be a lot of debate whether the 360-day calendar was for religious reasons or civil reasons, so I will continue as the Bible led, leaving the original ancient Hebrew calendar at 360 days.

Comparing the Feasts of Month One to Jesus' Last Days

Once I had the ancient Hebrew calendar complete, I began to look at the last days of Christ and place them on the calendar. Even though I had heard sermons and read literature about Christ being the Passover Lamb and being called the Firstfruits, I did not fully realize He was in step with the ancient Hebrew calendar.

	Day 1	Day 2	Day 3	Day 4	Day 5	Day 6	Sabbath
						1 New Moon	2
	3	4	5	6	7	8	9 Mary anoints the feet of Jesus
Month 1 (Abib / Nissan)	10 Lamb selected Jesus selected King	11 Jesus' head anointed Plot to kill Jesus	12	13	14 Last Supper Jesus' arrest Preparation Day Jesus' trials and crucifixion	15 Full Moon Passover Feast High Day / Sabbath	16
	17 Firstfruit Resurrection Male lamb slain	18	19	20	21 End of Passover	22	23 Sabbath 1
	24	25	26	27	28	29	30 Sabbath 2

I had spent a lot of time trying to figure out the number of days in a year, whether 360 days or our current calendar of 365.25, but I was missing the bigger picture. Christ fulfilled and will fulfill the ancient Hebrew calendar. For the first month, I placed the steps of Jesus on to the calendar. Here are the results:

Symbolic References in the First Month

- Day 10: Jesus is selected King on Palm Sunday, the same day the lamb is selected for the Seder meal.

- The lamb remains with the family for three and a half days before being slain. Although not stated in the Bible, theologians suggest Jesus' ministry and time with his apostles lasted for three and a half years.

- As the Passover lamb is inspected and found without blemish, Jesus is inspected three times and found without fault.

- The priest did not slay the Passover lamb. The lamb (or two) was taken to the temple by a member of a group of ten or twenty; that same individual would kill the lamb once there.[40] The priest would sprinkle the blood on the altar afterward.

- As Passover lambs are selected and killed by the congregation, Jesus was selected and condemned to be crucified by a congregation of people.

- The crucifixion of Jesus was between the third and ninth hour. The daily, continual sacrifice of the lambs occurred in the morning and evening.

- The day Jesus was crucified was also called Preparation Day, for the upcoming Feast of Unleavened Bread. Jesus' body was "prepared," wrapped in linen and placed in a tomb.

- Jesus was in the tomb for three days and nights.

- On the day of Firstfruits, which is the first of the grain harvest, Jesus is resurrected and the first "harvest" of the saints occurs.

"And the graves were opened; and many bodies of the saints which slept arose."

—Matthew 27:52 KJV

- The Bible specifically calls for a **male** lamb to be sacrificed and the blood sprinkled on the altar after the Firstfruit's wave offering. Read what Jesus told Mary on Resurrection Day:

"Touch me not; for I am not yet ascended to my Father, but go to my brethren, and say unto them, I ascend unto my Father, and your Father, and to my God and your God."

—John 20:17 NKJV

- Jesus was the **Male** Lamb sacrifice after the Firstfruits of the resurrection of the old saints were "waved" before God. Jesus, being the High Priest, sprinkled His blood on the altar of God.

Tying Jesus to the first month was a revealing that left me awestruck.

The final first month occurrence to investigate is the solar eclipse on March 19, 33 AD, which lined up with the country of Israel between the 9:35 a.m. (sixth hour) and 12:01 p.m. (ninth hour). On NASA's website, they noted that this eclipse may have been the crucifixion of Jesus. I have read arguments supporting a physical and a supernatural eclipse. From the passage in Luke 23:44,

> "And it was about the sixth hour, and there was darkness over all the earth until the ninth hour."

From the ordinances of the heavens you have learned and the review of the feast and construction of the calendar, can you prove or disprove the darkness experienced during the crucifixion occurred during a solar eclipse? During a solar eclipse, where is the position of the moon, and what phase does it have?

A solar eclipse occurs during a new moon, which is the first day of the month for the Hebrew calendar. Jesus was crucified on the fourteenth day of the first month, which could have been the day of—or one or two days before—a full moon. Therefore, the darkness as witnessed and reported by the four Gospels could not have been a solar eclipse, but supernatural. Furthermore, the position calculated by NASA would have cast a shadow of darkness on the lower African continent alone.

If 33 AD was the year Jesus was crucified as some calculate, the date of the crucifixion, using the Gregorian calendar, would be calculated as follows. The new moon and solar eclipse on March 19 would be the first day of Nisan, formerly Abib. The fourteenth of Nisan would fall on April 1, in which the sun would also be positioned in the constellation Aries, the lamb.

The following is speculation, but it's ironic, to say the least. What do we identify with the first day in April? April Fools' Day. Being curious, I researched the origin of April Fools' Day. I soon found the origin is not really known. According to the History Channel's "This Day in History," "Although the day, also called All Fools' Day, has been celebrated for several centuries by different cultures, its exact origins remain a mystery."[41]

The wheels inside my head began to turn: why is this day so mysterious, when it's just a silly day on which we play pranks? One explanation deals with the change to the Gregorian calendar in 1563 AD, and moving the date of the New Year from the spring equinox to January 1. The general public was confused about which day the New Year began, so the pranks of April's fools began.

The acknowledgement of this day also dates back to Constantinople, so where did this day actually originate? If Christ was crucified on the day we call April Fools, are we celebrating the day of the biggest trick on Satan?

Comparing the Feasts of Month Three

The third month is the Feast of Weeks, which is the day of Pentecost. The Apostles receive the Holy Spirit on this day.

Comparing the Feasts of Month Seven to the Last Days

Finally, let's look at the symbolism of the seventh month. As I mentioned earlier, God calls this the year end harvest, and the New Year begins. Since seven is a number meaning complete, and knowing the first month is symbolic for the beginning of Christianity, then the seventh month may be symbolic for the completion of God's plan. Today Hebrews call month seven the ecclesiastical year, and their civil year begins on Rosh Hashanah, the Feast of Trumpets.[42]

I use the word symbolism for month seven to comply with Scriptures, for no one knows the day. We may know the season, but not the day.

"Now learn a parable of the fig tree, when her branch is yet tender and putteth forth leaves, ye know that summer is near."

—Matthew 24:32 KJV

"But of that day and that hour knoweth no man, no, not the angels which are in heaven, neither the Son, but the Father."

—Mark 13:32

	Day 1	Day 2	Day 3	Day 4	Day 5	Day 6	Sabbath
Month 7 (Ethanim / Tishri)				1 New Moon Feast of Trumpets (Christ Returns)	2	3	4
	5	6	7	8	9 Fasting	10 Day of Atonement (Judgment Day)	11
	12	13	14	15 Full Moon Sabbath Feast of Tabernacles (Marriage Feast)	16	17	18
	19	20	21 End of Feast	22 Sabbath Solemn Assembly	23	24	25
	26	27	28	29	30		

Here are the symbolic references I saw in month seven. Since these events have not yet happened, more than likely I have missed some, if not most, of the symbolism. I encourage you to do your own studies and find additional examples of symbolism. Knowing month seven applies to the year-end gathering, what do you see?

Symbolic References in the Seventh Month

Theories abound about the end times and its related sequence of events. I believe month seven has a relationship to the end, and the following are a few of the symbols I interpreted.

- Some have theorized Jesus was born on the Feast of Trumpets; however, in my brief study, I calculated His birth occurred in the summer.

- The Hebrews consider the Feast of Trumpets to be a Day of Judgment; it is also a day where trumpets are blown throughout the land. I think this is symbolic with Christ's return, as the following verse suggests.

"In a moment, in the twinkling of an eye, at the **last trump**: for the trumpet shall sound, and the dead shall be raised incorruptible, and we shall be changed."

—1 Corinthians 15:52 KJV (emphasis mine)

- I have not understood the Bible to state that Christ returns the day before the seven-year period of Great Tribulation; however, His return is with the sound of a trumpet. The Day of Trumpets actually "sounds" to be symbolic for this event.

- The Day of Atonement is a day of cleaning and purification. Does this day symbolize the purging of the world of sin and then the Judgment?

- The Day of Atonement with the Jubilee trumpet could mark the end of an age, the awesome and terrible Day of the Lord.

"Immediately after the tribulation of those days shall the sun be darkened, and the moon shall not give her light, and the stars shall fall from heaven, and the powers of the heavens shall be shaken. And then shall appear the sign of the Son of man in heaven: and then shall all the tribes of the earth mourn, and they shall see the Son of man coming in the clouds of heaven with power and great glory. And he shall send his angels with a **great sound of a trumpet**, and they shall gather together his elect from the four winds, from one end of heaven to the other."

—Matthew 24:29–31 (emphasis mine)

"And it shall come to pass in that day, that **the great trumpet** shall be blown, and they shall come which were ready to perish in the land of Assyria, and the outcasts in the land of Egypt, and shall worship the LORD in the holy mount at Jerusalem."

—Isaiah 27:13 (emphasis mine)

- The Feast of Tabernacles lasts seven days, and traditional Jewish weddings lasted seven days. I associated this feast with the marriage supper of the Lamb (Christ).

- During the millennium reign of Christ, the Feast of Tabernacles will still be celebrated.

- I mentioned earlier to pay attention to the number of sacrifices slain during the Feast of Tabernacles; all four types are multiples of seven, for completion. Since forty-nine lambs are slain, I believe the Jubilee Trumpet, blown to free slaves and erase debts, for the fiftieth year is symbolic for Jesus being the fiftieth Lamb, setting us free from our sin debt with the destruction of the Devil.

- Finally, seventy young bulls are slain, which I believe to be symbolic for the fulfillment of Daniel's missing seventieth week.

"Seventy weeks are determined upon thy people and upon thy holy city, to finish the transgression, and to make an end of sins, and to make reconciliation for iniquity, and to bring in everlasting righteousness, and to seal up the vision and prophecy, and to anoint the most Holy."

—Daniel 9:24

Now that we have some symbolism for month seven, does this mean we will know the day of the Lord's return? No. We are not on God's calendar, which only He knows. The calendar systems of the world have been changed several times, so calculating or even approximating is futile.

Based on the little amount of research I completed on the various calendars, I am bewildered, even today, in the different types used. I have done sufficient studying on the construction of calendars and the astronomy behind these calendars to shake my head when someone calculates the second coming of Jesus. For me, the variations in all the calendars confirm that no one knows the day, not even the year.

In the beginning, God created the lights (stars) to signify signs, seasons, days, and years. In this section of the book, I have demonstrated how stars can be used for determining seasons (Earth's position with the twelve con-stellations), the beginning of a day (first visible star), and to measure a year (fixating upon a constellation or star). Now we will venture into how those bright shining objects were physically used for signs, continuing our search for the Mazzaroth.

The Birth of a Nation

"Blessed is the nation whose God is the LORD;
and the people whom he hath chosen for his own inheritance."

—Psalm 33:12 KJV

In the previous section of this book, I showed some basics of astronomy to provide some background, and touched on some of my thoughts on the Mazzaroth. The twelve main constellations along Earth's ecliptic were identified along with how they may have been used for determining when particular seasons of the year were approaching.

Now we have a basic understanding of astronomy; we've identified the twelve main constellations, where to find them, and an accepted pattern used today. The second half of this book will propose how their patterns are described in the Bible and demonstrate the application of the twelve constellations to the birth of the nation Israel.

The remainder of this adventure will also provide more evidence that before God created those twinkling stars in the night sky, he knew the end from the beginning.

After the Great Flood, civilizations, land, and fowl animals have been destroyed, leaving a small remnant of survivors in a large boat, called an ark, to repopulate the planet. After the flood, the survivors begin to settle down and start the rest of their lives. After an intoxicating event, and sobriety sets in, Noah begins to prophesy to his three sons.

While I was conducting this particular phase of my research, the following was not on my radar. But when reviewing the genealogy of Shem in a different study, the following verse took on new meaning. Shem would be the family bloodline from Noah, leading to the formation of Israel.

"God shall enlarge Japheth, and **he** shall dwell in the tents of Shem . . ."

—Genesis 9:27 (emphasis mine)

At first reading, it sounds like Japheth would live in the tents of Shem. This is a frustrating part of pronouns in the Bible; sometimes they can be confusing. Knowing the outcome for the lineage of Shem, this verse took on a prophetic meaning. Read the verse again, replacing "he" with God. While the children of Israel are in the wilderness dwelling in tents, God would also dwell in a tent, called a tabernacle.

After writing the above, I looked at how other Bible translations translated this verse, replacing the word "he" with Japheth or him. Looking at the Hebrew language, it was not clear to me. There is no evidence in the Bible where I read Japheth dwelled in the tents of Shem, for Japheth's descendants moved north into or near modern-day Turkey. I may be incorrect in my conclusion that the pronoun "he" could be God, but I thought it was interesting to point out.

The lineage of Shem will lead to a man named Abram, whose name will be changed to Abraham. God will give him a promise and a motto, which will be uttered multiple times.

"And I will make of thee a great nation . . . And I will bless them that bless thee, and curse him that curseth thee."

—Genesis 12:2, 3

It is worth noting Jesus will change this motto for Christianity:

"[B]less them that curse you."

—Luke 6:28 (brackets mine)

God blesses Abraham's wife, Sarai, changing her name to Sarah. Read the blessing carefully for the prediction of the future generations of her son, Isaac.

"[S]he shall be a mother of nations; kings of people shall be of her."

—Genesis 17:16

The future generations of Sarah will be nations, plural, for the divided kingdom, Israel and Judah, and the kings ruling the divided kingdom will be from her. God's intended purpose was for Israel to be united, not having a king, with only Him as their King; however, they wanted to be under a monarchy like their neighboring countries. This two-part prophecy was fulfilled approximately 1,300 to 1,400 years in the future (depending on how the years are measured), so it, too, can be added to the evidence that God knew the end from the beginning.

As Isaac grows he too will receive a blessing from God.

"I will be with you and bless you; for to you and your descendants I give all these
lands, and I will perform the oath which I swore to Abraham your father.
And I will make your descendants multiply as the stars of heaven;
I will give to your descendants all these lands; and in your seed all the nations
of the earth shall be blessed."

—Genesis 26:3–4

This blessing of God continues to be fulfilled even in our time. The descendants of Isaac have been on the brink of extinction, exiled, held in captivity and scattered a few times in their history, yet a remnant has always survived and repopulated. The descendants continue to bless the nations today. Can you think of ways the nations are blessed? Do the following individuals ring a bell?

Jesus Christ. Jesus has blessed all nations above all, and one could say the blessing of Isaac was solely for the Savior of the World.

Look back at history of the famous people and their influence in the world, even today:

Dr. Ernst Chain, a biochemist, who further developed penicillin for use as a medicine.[43]

Sigmund Freud, Albert Einstein, those in the women's suffrage movement, singers, Hollywood actors, etc.

Looking at the winners of the Nobel Prizes, the Jewish population makes up 0.2 percent of the population of the world yet has claim to around 40 percent of the Nobel Prizes in Economics and numerous Nobel Prizes in other categories.[44] Studying the contributions of Jewish people in the world, you will see how richly they have blessed the world.

Continuing on, Isaac and Rebekah will have twins, Esau and Jacob. The Lord foretells Rebekah, of whom the firstborn, Esau, will serve his twin brother Jacob. As the boys grew, Esau became a hunter and outdoorsman, while Jacob dwelled in tents. I picture Jacob being a studious and curious man, and I wonder if the picture show in the night sky intrigued him. Jacob dwelling in tents could also be foreshadowing the nation's fate.

Three hundred and fifty-three years after Shem received his blessing, Jacob is born, who will go on to have twelve sons. Later on in Jacob's life, he will wrestle with an angel, who will redeem him and change his name to Israel (Yisrael), meaning "God Prevails."

The Hebrew primitive root of Yisra, Sarah (Strong's Number 08280),[45] also means power, so the name Israel can have a deeper sense as "the Power of God." This is the origin from which the name of the nation is derived, yet the tribes of Israel will be formed from the twelve sons Jacob sired.

Jacob had one son, Joseph, who was favored amongst all the children. This favoritism caused resentment between the sons of Jacob. Their resentment grew even deeper when Joseph told his brother and father of his prophetic dreams.

Joseph's Second Dream

In the story of Joseph, he had a dream of eleven stars, the sun and moon bowing down to him. This dream will be the basis on which this portion of the book is hinged. As Joseph tells his dream, his father, Jacob, rebukes him, saying,

> "Shall I and thy mother and thy brethren indeed come to bow down ourselves to thee to the earth?"
>
> —Genesis 37:10 KJV

We gain something important from this statement. Jacob is allowing us to see his background and his exposure to astral philosophies of that day. It is important to note that Jacob has knowledge of the stars and their representations; however, there is a flaw in Jacob's interpretation of Joseph's dream.

The prophecy of Joseph's dream is fulfilled . . . almost. The eleven stars, or constellations, are for the eleven brothers of Joseph, who bowed down to him in Egypt. Joseph is the twelfth constellation.

Jacob considers the sun to represent his father and the moon to signify his mother; however, using Jacob's analogy yields to an incomplete prophecy, for Rachel died giving birth to Benjamin. This left me wondering: who was the moon that bowed down to Joseph in Egypt?

The moon could be for Leah, his stepmother; however, Leah died before Jacob moved to Egypt. The representative for the moon did not bow down to Joseph, or did she (or he)? Was there a flaw in Joseph's prophecy?

I pondered over this dilemma in prophecy for three weeks. One weekend, I was with my younger son at a birthday party. He wanted to play a pinball machine, but being three years old, he could not quite reach and see. After I let him press the buttons and pull the lever back a few times, his curiosity was satisfied and he went on to do something else. As I walked away from the machine, God revealed to me the moon was Jacob. Puzzled, I immediately asked, "Who was the sun? The answer came just as quickly, "Israel."

The wheels inside my head began to turn, and when I got home, I wrote down the following: *I need to understand the reasons Jacob and Israel are used in the same verses.* Throughout the Bible the two names are used almost interchangeably, but there is a significance when one name is used and when the other is present.

As I read verses where both names appear, I began to understand. I reasoned that when the name Jacob is used, it represents the physical state; when the name "Israel" is used, it represents the spiritual state. With this key, the verses containing one or both of the names in the Bible became more meaningful.

To support the sun and moon analogy, the following came to mind. In sermons, Jacob has been referred to as the lesser man; Israel, the greater man.

> "And God made two great lights; the greater light to rule the day [the sun], and the lesser light to rule the night [the moon]: he made the stars also."
>
> —Genesis 1:16 (brackets mine)

In Joseph's dream, there are eleven stars or constellations, plus Joseph's star. This may represent the twelve main constellations along Earth's elliptic. Throughout the course of my research, I found the following definition of a constellation in the 1906 Jewish Encyclopedia:

> "The twelve constellations represent the twelve tribes, while each station of the zodiac has thirty paths, and each path has thirty legions [of stars] (Ber. 32b). The standards of the tribes corresponded to the zodiacal signs of the constellations . . ."[46]

Is it possible the constellations assigned to each tribe can be found in the Bible? This is a strange concept I had never heard, yet I have only seen few constellations mentioned in the Bible. Identifying the constellation associated with each son and tribe will certainly be a challenge. However, I will present clues from the Bible to identify the pattern of the constellation for each son and tribe, and show what may have been used on their banners in the wilderness.

Blessings and Hidden Constellations

On a long drive to visit my parents, I was pondering over this portion of book, on how to make it more enjoyable for you. I decided to present the ancient clues and allow you to assign the constellation to each tribe. If you successfully do so, you will see a symbolism at the tabernacle and in the nighttime sky. You only have to get four key tribes correct . . . and three of them are pretty obvious.

This will not be an easy task, for the constellations are found in three places and are not given the same pattern. You will have to go inside the head of an ancient charlatan, Jacob, to view the patterns in his eyes of the nightly scene in the sky. Second, you will have to get inside the head of a famous ancient sorcerer, Balaam, to understand what he saw on the banners of each tribe of Israel. Finally, you will have to go inside the head of Moses, a former prince and murderer, who performed many miracles to free his people and spent many years talking directly with God.

Allow me to set the scenes for you. As each child is born, there is a birth announcement that defines the name of the child. Also notice that in each child's birth, the Lord or God or some acknowledgement of Divinity is used in most of the children's announcements, except one. This exception will be prophetic five hundred years later.

The second scene has an aging Jacob on his deathbed in Egypt. He calls together all his sons and blesses them. His blessings are both poetic and prophetic, foreshadowing Christ, and give insight into the ensign that will be used on the banners in the wilderness. Jacob does not tell you

the constellation, but he does provide the pattern he identified with each son in the night sky.

The third scene occurs in the wilderness on top of hills and mountains. As the children of Israel are encroaching upon the Promised Land, Balak, king of the Moabites, becomes troubled after hearing of the destruction of the Amorites. He comes up with the idea to use divination to curse the children of Israel, protecting his kingdom from destruction. He will hire a famous pagan of the time, Balaam, known for his sorcery and ability to curse people, to place a curse on the children of Israel; however, Balaam instead will be used by God to bless the tribes.

In four different locations and five attempts, Balak's plan to curse the children of Israel will fail. During these attempted curses, Balaam will be positioned where he sees the tribes and their banners, and the spirit of God will come upon him. Reading through Balaam's blessings, I realized he described the banners; however, to add to the mystery, the individual tribe is not identified.

"And Balaam lifted up his eyes, and he saw Israel abiding in his tents according to their tribes; and the spirit of God came upon him."

—Numbers 24:2 KJV

The blessings of Balaam are prophetic, prophesizing Christ and events of things to come, and provide description for the images on the banners. There are similarities in Jacob and Balaam's blessing that will aid in deciphering which tribe Balaam is describing. Although Balaam is used by God to bless the future nation of Israel, he will later be killed by the hands of the children of Israel.

The last scene comes from Moses when he is near death. He will bless each tribe, providing their land inheritance, their future, and perhaps their future industry. He may reference their banner and the constellation assignment.

However, one big question remains: how do we know the constellation of the tribes were on the banners or associated with the banners?

After the children of Israel spent four hundred thirty years in Egypt, God will send Moses to lead them out of captivity. In the wilderness, God gave instructions for the building of His tabernacle, the position of the camping arrangement for the tribes with respect to the tabernacle, and the requirement for the tribes to camp by their ensign.

God tells Moses,

"Every man of the children of Israel shall pitch by his own standard, with the **ensign** of their father's house: far off about the tabernacle of the congregation shall they pitch."

—Numbers 2:2 (emphasis mine)

I placed emphasis on the word "ensign," for the Hebrew word is *'owth*. Let's read the creation story for the purpose of the stars.

"[T]he stars are for **signs**, seasons, days and years."

—Genesis 1:14 (emphasis and brackets mine)

Here I placed emphasis on the word "signs," or "'owth," in Hebrew. According to the Strong Numbers, 'owth can mean:

- sign, signal

- distinguishing mark

- banner

- remembrance

- miraculous sign

- omen

- warning

- token, ensign, standard, miracle, proof[47]

With the use of the word "'owth," these two verses provide a clue that the tribes of Israel have a relationship with a constellation, placing an identifying symbol on their banners. After spending many months researching, studying, and praying, I have almost convinced myself that the image on the banners was of their constellation and not the nice, pretty, well-designed banners we see today for the tribes.

These people were in the wilderness, and although they were rather skilled, I do not feel they were capable of printing exquisite artistic impressions on their banners. I have read arguments from rabbis who could not understand why God would tell them to place images on their banners when they were commanded not to create graven images. Surely, God did not want the golden calf incident again, and ironically, one of the tribes would have a bull.

For these reasons and the use of 'owth for banners applied to the stars,

I believe the tribes placed their constellation on their flags (which would have been easier to fabricate) and gives reason why the identification of

the patterns differ between Jacob, Balaam, and Moses. This would also satisfy the concerns the rabbis had about banner images.

Without further ado, let's begin our adventure through the twelve tribes. To begin identifying the tribes, we'll use the model from the astronomy section. We will start by applying the known information from Joseph's dream. Since I have provided the common pattern used today, the pages following our model will present the stars making up the constellation with the image outlines. This will give you the view of all the stars, and hopefully, the imagination to see the constellations from the ancients point of view.

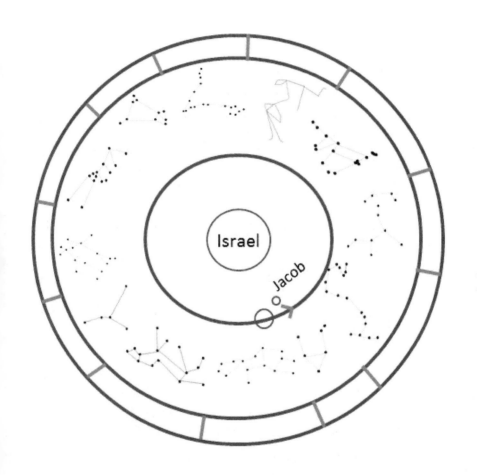

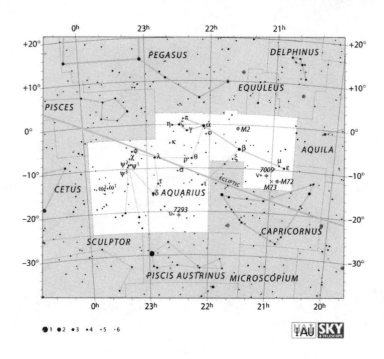

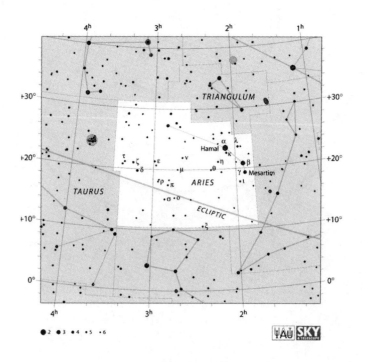

Aquarius and Aries

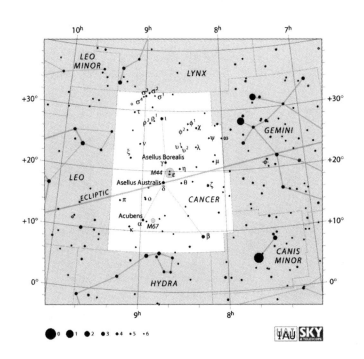

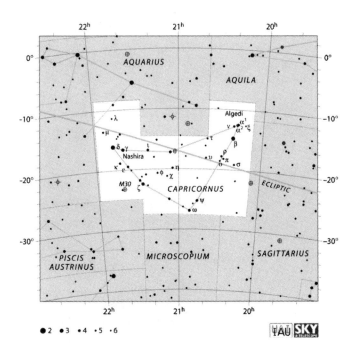

Cancer and Capricorn

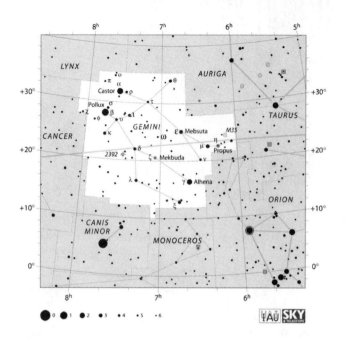

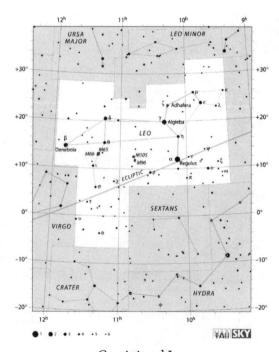

Gemini and Leo

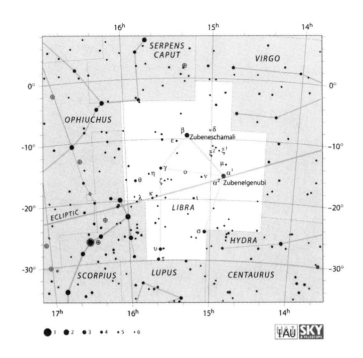

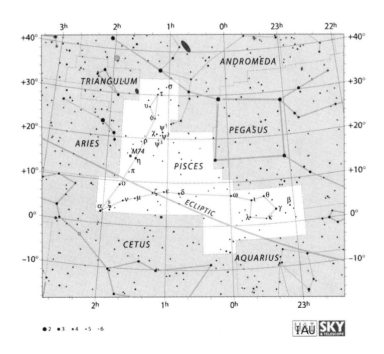

Libra and Pisces

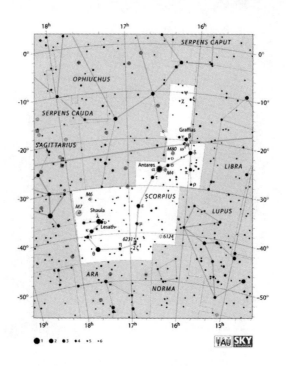

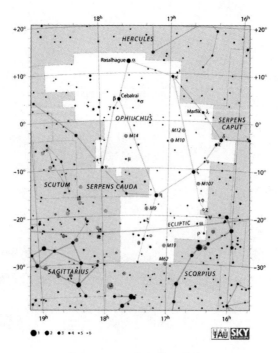

Scorpius and Ophiuchus

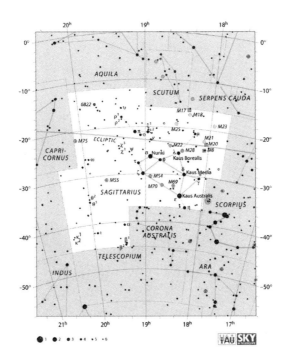

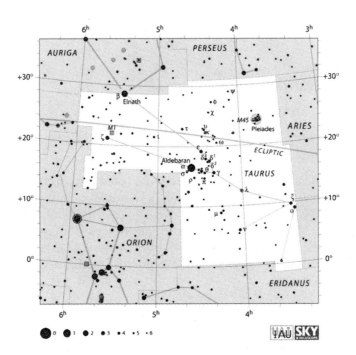

Sagittarius and Taurus

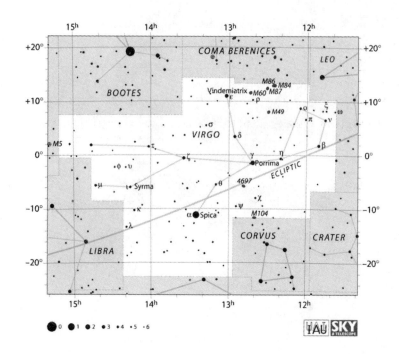

Virgo

Reuben (Re'uwben) – See a Son

Reuben is the first born, and Leah announces,

> "Surely the **Lord** hath looked upon my **affliction**; now my husband will love me."
>
> —Genesis 29:32 KJV (emphasis mine)

The word "affliction" is used for women who could not conceive, for children were considered blessings of God. Leah expresses this word, for the birth of the Reuben was surely from the Lord. She had been married to Jacob for more than seven years before having a child. Adding to the stress of being fruitless, she was unloved by Jacob. Her sister, Rachel, being the love of Jacob's life, imbues Leah with a desire to have children, attempting to gain Jacob's love.

As we look at each child, you may get a sense of the competition between the two sisters vying for Jacob's love. As Jacob nears death, a clue emerges as to whom he ultimately chose.

In looking for clues to assign Reuben a constellation, we don't discover anything in Leah's birth announcement. Also note that Leah uses the word "Lord" in her announcement.

As we turn to the next location to search for a constellation, Jacob blessed Reuben with:

> "**Unstable as water**, thou shalt not excel; because thou wentest up to thy father's bed; then defiledst thou it: he went up to my couch."
>
> —Genesis 49:4 (emphasis mine)

Jacob blesses Reuben using a key reference, "Unstable as water." This is an odd reference, and our first clue to identifying Reuben's constellation. The Douay-Rheims Bible uses the phrase "poured out as water" (Gen. 49:4). Studying the entire blessing of Reuben further, you may see a reference to Christ. The next blessing will provide another clue.

In Balaam's second blessing, he appears to be looking at Reuben's banner and starts with,

> "God is not **a man,** that he should lie, nor a **son** of **man** . . ."
>
> —Numbers 23:19

Balaam's third blessing reads,

> "[H]e shall **pour the water out of his buckets, and his seed shall be in many waters** . . ."
>
> —Numbers 24:7 (emphasis and brackets mine)

This is a rather odd phrase, but it also provides a significant clue.

Finally, Moses blesses the tribe of Reuben with,

> "[A]nd let not **his men** be few."
>
> —Deuteronomy 33:6 (emphasis and brackets mine)

For Reuben, what constellation features the act of pouring water from a bucket and a man?

Simeon (Shim'own) – Heard

Simeon is the second born of Leah, and she announces,

> "Because the **Lord** has **heard** that I am unloved"
>
> —Genesis 29:33 NKJV (emphasis mine)

Leah expresses her gratitude, continuing her desire to be loved by Jacob.

Jacob blesses Simeon and Levi together with,

> "Simeon and Levi are brethren; **instruments** of cruelty are in their **habitations**
> be not thou **united**."

> —Genesis 49:5 KJV (emphasis mine)

The Hebrew word for instruments, Kaeliy, in this sense means weapon of war; and the Hebrew word for habitations, *Maekerah,* represents swords in the sense of stabbing. Is there a constellation with a star pattern that can be identified with swords?

For Balaam, I did not find any reference to a constellation, but interestingly enough, he mentioned valleys in the third blessing.

Oddly, Moses leaves out the tribe of Simeon in his blessing.

This constellation assignment is not as clear as Reuben's. Rabbis in the past have assigned the same constellation to Simeon and Levi; however, this goes against Joseph's dream of eleven stars bowing down. To assist you further, in which constellation pattern can you make out two swords or a valley? When looking at the constellations, which constellation(s) have two things united?

Levi (Leviy) – Joined to, United

Levi is the third son of Leah, and she exclaims,

> "Now this time will my husband **be joined** unto me."

> —Genesis 29:34 KJV (emphasis mine)

Notice what is left out. There is no reference to the Lord or God, and I find this curious and perhaps prophetic. As we conclude with the sons, I will make a summary of the birth announcements and the reason I think this is prophetic.

Jacob blesses Simeon and Levi together with,

> "Simeon and Levi are brethren; **instruments** of cruelty are in their **habitations** . .
> . be not thou **united**."

> —Genesis 49:5 (emphasis mine)

The following blessing from Balaam is where I saw something interesting in one of the constellations.

"A **Star** shall rise out of Jacob, and a Scepter out of Israel."

—Numbers 24:17 (emphasis mine)

This part of the blessing, often used at Christmastime, foretold of the coming Messiah. Revisiting Joseph's dream, I mentioned that when Jacob and Israel are used in the same verse, I read Jacob as physical and Israel as spiritual. For me, this verse implies a star to be physical—there was a star to announce the birth of Jesus—yet the Scepter represents the spiritual King rising out of Israel.

Moses gives a lengthy blessing for Levi, which is responsible for the priesthood. I did not find any clues to a constellation in his blessing, for most of the blessing concerned Levi's responsibilities. At the beginning of the blessing, Moses makes note of a peculiar item that would be lost after the destruction of the first temple.

"Let your Thummin and your Urim be with your holy one."

—Deuteronomy 33:8

Many theories abound over what these two objects actually are—a pair of dice, a black and white stone—and some believe they may have been related to the Star of David, but we do not know. Unfortunately, this is a lost relic.

For the tribe of Levi, we have clues of "joined," "united," and "a star."

Judah (Yehuwdah) – Praise

Judah is the fourth son of Leah, and she proclaims,

"Now will I **praise** the **LORD**."

—Genesis 29:35 KJV (emphasis mine)

Placing Judah as the fourth son unlocked a significance found in Leviticus 19:23. When the Israelites came into the Promised Land and planted all manner of trees, the first three years are counted uncircumcised, and the **fourth** year of all fruit shall be holy to **praise** the Lord.

The first three sons of Jacob committed acts where they lost the birthright synonymous for uncircumcised. The Bible tells of Judah's issues, yet his repentant heart allows him to be granted the birthright, leaving the **fourth** son holy to **praise** to the Lord.

Jacob gives a rather lengthy blessing for Judah, who receives the birthright. Targum texts differ, saying Judah receives the kingdom, Joseph the birthright, and Levi the priesthood.

Judah will be an important tribe carrying the lineage of Christ, and his lengthy prophetical blessing points to the birth of Christ and the second return. In clues related to the constellations, Jacob says,

> "Judah is a **lion's whelp** . . . he couched as a **lion**, and as an **old lion [lioness]** . . ."
>
> —Genesis 49:9 (emphasis and brackets mine)

Jacob uses a lion's whelp to identify Judah as the beginning, a young lion cub that will grow and be the lineage of Christ, the Great Lion.

One of my favorite lines in all of Jacob's blessing is the following for Judah:

> "Binding his foal unto the vine, and his ass's colt unto the choice vine . . ."
>
> —Genesis 49:11

This is a two-part prophecy of Jesus Christ. The first is the prophecy of Jesus riding on an ass's colt on Palm Sunday. Second, the Hebrew word for binding provides the sense of beginning the battle. Jesus began the battle by binding into the vine of Abraham, Isaac, and Jacob, and unto the choice vine, the vine of Judah. When we accept Christ, we are also grafted to the choice vine.

Tragically, the Jewish Targums I read omitted this line of Jacob's blessing. This became a common occurrence I picked up on when reading the Targums. When there is a reference to the first time Jesus was on the earth, the Targums omit the lines, do not expound upon it, or align it to an historical figure.

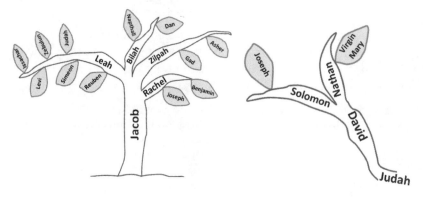

The Vine   The Choice Vine

In Balaam's second attempt to curse Israel, he says,

> "Behold, the people shall rise up as a **great lion**, and lift up himself as **a young lion.**

—Numbers 23:24 (emphasis mine)

In his third blessing, he reiterates the sentiment:

> "He couched, he lay down as a **lion**, and as a **great lion** . . ."

—Numbers 24:9 (emphasis mine)

This constellation assignment is straightforward, for which constellation is in the pattern of a lion?

Dan (Dan) – A Judge

Leah has given Jacob four sons. Rachel, feeling the pressure to provide a child for Jacob, offers her handmaiden Bilhah. Bilhah conceives and bares Jacob a son. At his birth, Rachel proclaims,

> "God hath **judged** me, and hath also heard my voice . . ."

—Genesis 30:6 KJV (emphasis mine)

Jacob blesses Dan in the following way:

> "Dan shall **judge** his people, as one of the tribes of Israel Dan shall be a **serpent by the way, a viper by the path that bites the horse's heels** so that its **rider shall fall backward.**"

—Genesis 49:16–17 NKJV (emphasis mine)

Moses gives his blessing:

> "And of Dan he said, Dan is a **lion's whelp**: he shall leap from Bashan."

—Deuteronomy 33:22 KJV (emphasis mine)

Balaam turns away from the tribes to face the Kenites and says,

> "[A]nd your **nest** is set in the **rock.**"

—Numbers 24:21 (emphasis and brackets mine)

Both Jacob and Rachel emphasize the action of judging for Dan, but only one known judge came from this tribe, Samson. Along the same lines, the prophet Jeremiah speaks of a voice coming from the land of Dan, for the judgment of God was impending upon Jerusalem.

Dan is a special tribe for me, for when I read Jacob's blessing, I had his constellation on my computer screen. At this point I realized that in some of

Jacob's blessing, he was identifying the constellations. Having been blessed to unlock this mystery, the blessings of the other children became more coherent.

In which constellation can you make out a snake striking a horse's heel, a lion, or an animal that sets its nest in the rocks? The last pattern is of the utmost significance.

Napthali (Napthaliy) – Wrestling

Naphtali, the second son by Rachel's handmaiden Bilhah, will be the sixth son of Jacob. Rachel's blessing states,

> "With **great wrestlings** have I **wrestled** with my sister, and I have prevailed."
>
> —Genesis 30:8 KJV (emphasis mine)

The word "great" (in bold) is the same Hebrew word for God, *Elohiym*. I do not know what to do with the phrase, "God wrestlings," which may be why the translators choose to use the word "great," but I want to point out God was used in her announcement.

Jacob's blessing is short:

> "Naphtali is a hind [deer] let loose; he giveth goodly words."
>
> —Genesis 49:21 (brackets mine)

Unfortunately, Moses does not provide a clue into the constellation for Naphtali with his blessing:

> "O Naphtali, satisfied with favor, and full with the blessing of the LORD: possess thou the west and the south."
>
> —Deuteronomy 33:23

Balaam may elude to seeing this constellation on Naphtali's banner with,

> "[H]e hath as it were the strength of a unicorn [wild ox?]."
>
> —Numbers 24:8 (brackets mine)

Can you make out the pattern of a deer or unicorn in one of the twelve constellations?

Gad (Gad) – A Troop

Leah, seeing Rachel has used her handmaiden to give Jacob two sons, does the same and offers her handmaiden Zilpah. Zilpah conceives and bares the child, Gad, the seventh son of Jacob. Leah gives a rather short statement:

> "A **Troop cometh!**"
>
> —Genesis 30:11 (emphasis mine)

Although not spelled out literally, a troop, is also used for Christ. Continuing the same train of thought, Jacob blesses,

> "A **troop** shall overcome him, but he shall overcome at the last."
>
> —Genesis 49:19 (emphasis mine)

As our search for a constellation continues, Moses blesses,

> "Blessed be he that enlargeth Gad: he dwelleth as a lion, and teareth the arm with the crown of the head."
>
> —Deuteronomy 33:20

The tribe of Gad was one of the last tribes I identified, and I had to go back to the ancient Babylonians to identify the constellation. I am not fully sure about Gad's assignment, and fortunately this was not one of the key tribes. What constellation would you assign for a troop and a crown?

Asher (Asher) – Happy One

In the duel between sisters, Leah evens the children's score of handmaidens, offering Zilpah again to Jacob. Leah, feeling content, states,

> "I am **happy** for the daughters will call me blessed."
>
> —Genesis 30:13 KJV (emphasis mine)

Identifying the children where God or the Lord appear, Asher's blessing does not seem to reference God. At first I did not find any Hebrew reference for happy and God, yet the Targums used praise and blessed instead of happy. At the end of Moses blessing, he says,

> "Happy are you, O Israel."
>
> —Deuteronomy 33:29 NKJV

It appears that Asher's blessing was divine, and he will be included in our list where God or the Lord is recognized.

On to our next cabinet of clues with Jacob's blessing:

> "Out of Asher his bread shall be fat, and he shall yield **royal** dainties."
>
> —Genesis 49:20 KJV (emphasis mine)

Mention of royalty can be found in Balaam's third blessing:

> "His **king** shall be higher than Agag, and his **kingdom** shall be exalted."
>
> —Numbers 24:7 (emphasis mine)

In Moses' blessing, he says,

> "Let Asher be blessed with children; let him be acceptable to his brethren, and let him dip his foot in oil. Thy shoes [under thy shoes] shall be iron and brass; and as thy days, so shall thy strength be."
>
> —Deuteronomy 33:24–25 (brackets mine)

This is another constellation I struggled with; fortunately, this was not a key tribe to unlocking the mystery around the tabernacle. Which constellation would you assign to symbolize royal dainties and a king?

Issachar (Yissakar) – Recompense, Wages

After Rachel's handmaiden delivers two children, Leah continues conceiving and bares Jacob another son, Issachar. Leah confesses,

> "God hath given me my **wages**, because I have given my maiden to my husband: and she called his name Issachar."
>
> —Genesis 30:18 NKJV (emphasis mine)

Jacob provides a prophetic blessing for his son:

> "Issachar is a **strong ass** couching down between **two burdens**. And he saw that **rest** was good, and the land that it was pleasant; and bowed his shoulder to bear, and became a servant unto tribute."
>
> —Genesis 49:14–15 KJV (emphasis mine)

Moses adds his blessing:

> "And of Zebulun he said, Rejoice, Zebulun, in thy going out; and, Issachar, **in thy tents**. They shall call the people unto the mountain; there they shall offer sacrifices of righteousness: for they shall suck of the abundance of the seas, and of treasures hid in the sand."
>
> —Deuteronomy 33:18–19 (emphasis mine)

When I read Moses' blessing, I pictured the future jobs for the tribe of Issachar and maybe Zebulun. If this part of the blessing is physical, what industry sucks the treasures hidden in the sand and the seas? The oil industry. This may not be the intended meaning, but I can only think of the oil industry when I read this blessing.

For Issachar, in what constellation can you make out the pattern for a tent, a strong ass, or wages?

Zebulun (Zebuwlum) – Exalted

Other names in the Bible: Zebulon, Zabulon

Zebulun is Leah's sixth and last son and has basically sealed up the victory for giving Jacob the most sons. Now Jacob will love her, as she boasts,

> "God hath endued me with a good dowry; now will my husband **dwell** with me, because I have born him six sons: and she called his name Zebulun.

> —Genesis 30:20 KJV (emphasis mine)

Jacob blesses the child by saying,

> "Zebulun shall **dwell** at the haven of the sea; and he shall be for an haven of **ships**; and his borders shall be unto Zidon."

> —Genesis 49:13 (emphasis mine)

I saw one text replace Zidon with Zion, for initially, Zebulun was landlocked, but expanded its inheritance by conquering land on the Mediterranean Sea and the Sea of Galilee. I have not seen any indication that Zebulun possessed Zidon (now called Sidon) on any map or anywhere in the Bible.

Even Balaam sees the standard of Zebulun with his blessing:

> "And **ships** shall come from the coast of Chittim . . ."

> —Numbers 24:24 (emphasis mine)

Daniel also mentions ships coming from Chittim. Where is Chittim? Chittim is the isle of Cyprus.

Since this could be prophetic, I researched naval bases on Cyprus. Britain has an air force base and a naval base on Cyprus, and on February 25, 2015, during the writing of this book, Russia signed a long-awaited agreement with Cyprus to use their naval bases.

Finally, Moses blesses,

> "And of Zebulun he said, Rejoice, Zebulun, in thy going out . . ."

> —Deuteronomy 33:18

In which constellation could you make out the pattern of a ship or tie the constellation with the word "dwell"?

Joseph (Yowceph) –Jehovah Has Added

Joseph, the first born of Rachel, was the favored son of Jacob. When he is born, Rachel foretells,

> "The LORD shall **add** to me another son."

—Genesis 30:24 KJV (emphasis mine)

Joseph is the one who has the dream, giving us insight that the sons of Jacob are named after the twelve main constellations. Rachel's prophetic announcement will come true, and she will bare one more son.

Jacob gives us an interesting statement as he blesses Joseph:

> "Joseph is a fruitful **bough**, even a fruitful **bough** by a well, whose **branches** run over the wall."

—Genesis 49:22 (emphasis mine)

The Hebrew word used for bough is *ben*, which means son; branches is *bath*, meaning daughters. The translators chose to use the English word, bough, a main branch of a tree, and branches instead of daughters. This provides deeper insight into Jacob's view of the constellation of Joseph, where the same constellation will have two patterns, one for Ephraim and the other Manasseh.

The Targum of Onkelos expounds on vines as "two tribes will come forth from his son, and they shall receive a portion of the inheritance."[48]

Moses combines Ephraim and Manasseh in his blessing, and calls them the tribe of Joseph. He will provide us with the needed clue to identify the constellation of Joseph and the second pattern.

Moses says,

> "His glory is like the **firstling of his bullock**, and his horns are like the horns of unicorns (wild ox). And for the precious **fruits** brought forth by the sun, and for the **precious things** put forth by the moon."

—Deuteronomy 33:17 (emphasis mine)

Like Jacob, Moses also gives us the second pattern in the constellation, branches and vines. The sun brings forth the fruit on branches, and the moon the produce, precious things of the vine.

These two patterns will be passed on to each of Joseph's sons. Which constellations make the pattern of a bullock and can also make out a vine or branch splitting into two?

Ben-Oni, Benjamin – Son of My Sorrow, Son of My Right Hand

As Rachel foretold us at Joseph's birth, she has another son, Benjamin, her last son. She dies after having a hard labor, but in her dying words, she names her son "Ben-Oni," which means son of my sorrow. Jacob calls him Benjamin, "Son of my right hand." I think this is a referenced to Jesus, who sits on the right hand of the Father.

When it is time for the blessing, Jacob gives us a clue into Benjamin's constellation.

> "Benjamin shall ravin as a **wolf**: in the morning he shall devour the prey . . ."
>
> —Genesis 49:27 KJV (emphasis mine)

Balaam also reiterates in his second blessing,

> "It [Israel] shall not lie down until it devours the prey . . ."
>
> —Numbers 23:24 NKJV (brackets mine)

And in his third blessing,

> "He shall consume the nations, his enemies . . ."
>
> —Numbers 24:8

Moses blesses the tribe of Benjamin with,

> "The beloved of the LORD shall dwell in safety by him, and the Lord shall cover him all the day long, and he shall dwell **between his shoulders**."
>
> —Deuteronomy 33:12 KJV (emphasis mine)

If you have been going in order, your selections for constellations are limited. In which constellation would you make out the image of a wolf?

Manasseh (Menashsheh) – Forgetful

Manasseh is the firstborn of Joseph, and an accomplishment for Joseph. The joy of this child will make all the sorrows of his ordeals to be forgotten, for Joseph laments,

> "For God, said he, hath made me forget all my toil, and all my father's house."
>
> —Genesis 41:51 KJV

Jacob blesses Manasseh and Ephraim together, and places Ephraim on his right hand and Manasseh on his left hand. This is a sign that Manasseh loses the birthright. (More detail of the blessing and the interpretation is given in the section on Ephraim).

From Jacob's blessing of Joseph, the constellation is identified, and the pattern for Manasseh is given by Jacob and Moses.

> "Joseph is a fruitful **bough**, even a fruitful **bough** by a well ..."
>
> —Genesis 49:22 (emphasis mine)

Moses blesses,

"And for the **precious fruits** brought forth by the sun, and for the **precious things** put forth by the moon,"

> —Deuteronomy 33:14 (emphasis mine)

This statement can also be for Israel and Jacob.

Manasseh is given the pattern of a fruitful vine.

Ephraim (Ephrayim) – I Shall be Doubly Fruitful, Double Ash Heap

Joseph's Birth Announcement

> "For God hath caused me to be **fruitful** in the land of my affliction."
>
> —Genesis 41:52 KJV (emphasis mine)

Jacob's Blessing

> "Truly his younger brother (Ephraim) shall be greater than he (Manasseh), and his seed shall become a multitude of nations."
>
> —Genesis 48:19 (emphasis mine)

Moses' Blessing

> "His glory is like the **firstling of his bullock**, and his horns are like the horns of unicorns [wild ox]."
>
> —Deuteronomy 33:17 KJV (emphasis and brackets mine)

The children of Joseph are reversed when Jacob goes to bless them. There is no indication that Manasseh did anything wrong to lose the birthright, as Reuben, Simeon, and Levi had transgressed. Even Joseph tries to correct Jacob, but Jacob says,

> "I know it, my son ... he also shall become a people ..."
>
> —Genesis 48:18

Joseph has been identified with two patterns in the same constellation, although Ephraim's name is fruitful and the blessing eludes to a fruitful bough.

Summary of the Twelve Tribes

Now that each child has been reviewed, let's look at our summaries, starting with each child's birth announcement. I have highlighted which children reference God in their birth announcement and which one did not.

Tribe	Mother	Literal Meaning at Birth	Birth Announcement
Reuben	Leah	See, a Son	Surely the **LORD** hath looked upon my affliction; now therefore my husband will love me.
Simeon	Leah	Heard	Because the **LORD** hath heard that I was hated, he hath therefore given me this son also.
Levi	Leah	Joined	Now this time will my husband be joined unto me, because I have born him three sons.
Judah	Leah	Praise	Now will I praise the **LORD**.
Dan	Bilhah – Rachel	Judge	**God** hath judged me, and hath also heard my voice, and hath given me a son.
Naphtali	Bilhah – Rachel	Wrestling	With **Great (God)** wrestlings have I wrestled with my sister, and I have prevailed.
Gad	Zilpah – Leah	Troop of Fortune	A **troop cometh.**
Asher	Zilpah – Leah	Happy	**Happy** am I, for the **daughters** will call me **blessed.**
Issachar	Leah	Wages	**God** hath given me my hire, because I have given my maiden to my husband:
Zebulun Leah	Leah	Dwelling	**God** hath endued me with a good dowry; now will my husband dwell with me, because I have born him six sons.
Joseph Rachel	Rachel	He will add / fruitfulness	**God** hath taken away my reproach: The LORD shall add to me another son.

Ben Oni Benjamin	Rachel	Son of my Sorrow Son of my right hand	Ben Oni – **Son** of my sorrow. Benjamin – **Son** of my right hand.
Manasseh	Asenath	Making For- getful	For **God**, hath made me forget all my toil, and all my father's house.
Ephraim	Asenath	Fruitfulness	For **God** hath caused me to be fruitful in the land of my affliction.

There was no reference to God or the Lord in Levi's birth announcement, for it was carnal and self-centered. This may have significant, prophetic importance, for Levi would be the tribe to carry the priesthood of Israel and would not have a land inheritance.

Applying the Constellations

With each child and tribe, you have identified a constellation from biblical references. Many rabbis and others have tried to assign the constellations based on the zodiac signs to the twelve tribes; however, I have not seen where any looked up into the night sky where the "signs of the zodiac" originated.

Some used the zodiac wheel, making triangles, the four elements, and incorporating the birth order. Others used the Hebrew roots found in the Bible to assign the tribes to the constellations of the zodiac.

Once I understood the patterns of the constellations that were being described, the wording of the blessings did not seem so mysterious.

The following is an excerpt from the book *Mazzaroth*, written in 1862:

"Commentators also differ; some, however, have perceived the allusions to the twelve signs, as borne on the standards of Israel, but have not consistently explained or adapted them: not even the Jewish writers who inform us that they were so borne. However, these ancient authorities unanimously assert that Reuben bore Aquarius; Joseph, Taurus; Benjamin, Gemini under the symbol of a wolf, and Dan Scorpio under that of an Eagle, crowned serpent or basilisk."[49]

Let's compare your results to the results of others. I will identify the four key tribes.

	Your Results	Harry Golemon	Jona-than Ben Uzziel[50]	Jerah-meel[51]	Hillel ben David[52]	Rev. J.A. Seiss[53]	Frances Rolleston[54]
Reuben		Aquarius	Taurus	Taurus	Taurus	Aquarius	Aquarius
Simeon		Pisces		Virgo	Gemini	Pisces	Pisces
Gad		Aries		Capricorn	Sagit-tarius	Aries	Aries
Judah		Leo	Leo	Leo	Leo	Leo	Leo
Zebulun		Virgo		Sagittarius	Virgo	Virgo	Virgo
Issachar		Libra		Aires	Libra	Cancer	Cancer
Ephraim		Taurus	Aquar-ius	Gemini	Pisces	Taurus	Taurus
Benjamin		Cancer		Aquarius	Aries	Gemini	Gemini
Manasseh		Taurus		Libra	Pisces	Taurus	
Dan		Scorpio	Scorpio	Cancer	Scorpio	Scorpio	Scorpio
Asher		Sagittarius		Scorpio	Capricorn	Sagit-tarius	Sagittarius
Naphtali		Capricor-nus		Pisces	Aquarius	Capricor-nus	Capricornus
Levi		Gemini			Cancer	Libra	Pisces

Applying the results to our model, we derive the following:

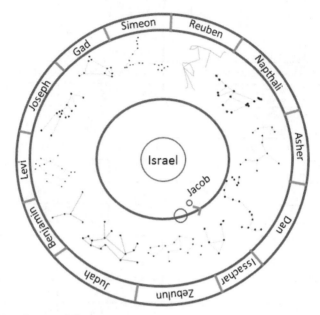

Layout in the Wilderness

Is there a way to check our model? God provides Moses very detailed instructions for the building of the tabernacle, the Ark of the Covenant, and for a specific camping arrangement around the tabernacle, with the instructions of being a good distance away.

> "Every man of the children of Israel shall pitch by his own standard, with the ensign of their father's house: far off about the tabernacle of the congregation shall they pitch."
>
> —Numbers 2:2 KJV

There are a few theories for the camping arrangement of the tribes around the tabernacle, and the layout may be of utmost significance. We are not told the exact arrangement, which is left to interpretation and can be miraculous and prophetic in itself.

In Numbers 2, God tells Moses that Judah will pitch toward the east; next to him shall be Issachar, then the tribe of Zebulun. On the south side is Reuben; next to him, Simeon; then Gad.

The tabernacle of the congregation will be in the midst of the camp of the Levites.

On the west side will be the camp of Ephraim; and by him, Manasseh; then Benjamin. Finally, on the north side will be the camp of Dan; and next to him, Asher; then Naphtali.

The size of the host, or army, is given, which can be used to estimate the population of each tribe. I believe the camping arrangement around the tabernacle has a significant representation, and with a little work from the two censuses, one can make out two significant imageries the tribes made.

There are varying opinions on the pattern the arrangement makes, such as a cross, a rectangle, a circle, and the Star of David. The children of Israel moved forty-two times in the wilderness, so there is the possibility that all the patterns were used, but I believe the most significant were the first and the last.

Studying the arrangement, taking the first census, conducted at the start of the wilderness experience, and the second census, taken at the end of forty years, created two models with the following in mind:

- We are not given the dimensions, only the size of each tribe and triad and the side of the tabernacle they encamp.

- We are given the triad under one standard.

- The layout had military significance to protect the tabernacle.

- Population expansion and decrease would have to be considered.

- The tribes would be close enough that Baalam could see their banners.

- The tribes broke camp in a determined order, marched in a specific order, and were mobile.

- The terrain would have to be considered, but for the purpose of the model, the assumption was made of nearly flat land in a 20 x 20 square mile sect.

- There was a mixed multitude and many animals with them on the journey.

Early in the book, I mentioned how engineers make models to understand process and how making models in the Bible will show us some interesting symbolism. I decided to create a model from the first and second census, estimating each family had a 10 x 10 foot lot, and using the number of people counted by Moses as a ratio. The model I created had mathematical significance.

The following tables are from the census of the tribes in descending order by population. Notice after forty years, the total population of the second census only changes by 1,070 people! This is highly intriguing, and a concept I do not fully grasp.

1st Census	
Judah	74,600
Dan	62,700
Simeon	59,300
Zebulon	57,400
Issachar	54,400
Naphtali	53,400
Reuben	46,500
Gad	45,600
Asher	41,500
Ephraim	40,500
Benjamin	35,400
Manasseh	32,200
Levi	22,300
Total	**625,800**

2nd Census	
Judah	76,500
Dan	64,400
Issachar	64,300
Zebulon	60,500
Asher	53,400
Manasseh	52,700
Benjamin	45,600
Naphtali	45,400
Reuben	43,730
Gad	40,500
Ephraim	32,500
Levi	23,000
Simeon	22,200
Total	**624,730**

The next table I created grouped the tribes—north and south, east and west—in triads positioned around the tabernacle and calculated the ratios.

Triad	1st Census	2nd Census
North	163,800	169,400
South	160,000	115,030
Ratio (N-S)	**1.024**	**1.473**

Triad	1st Census	2nd Census
East	186,400	201,300
West	115,396	138,300
Ratio (E-W)	**1.615**	**1.456**

We find in the first census that the tabernacle's location to the east and west tribes is 1.615, very close to a mathematical ratio of great importance, the golden ratio. Interestingly, the ratio of north to south is almost one. Laying out the tribes in this ratio provides an image of an aesthetical cross.

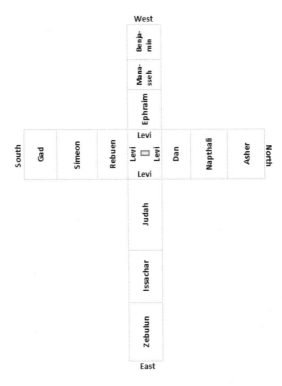

Do you now understand the reason Balaam had such a difficult time cursing the children of Israel? In scanning through TV stations, I paused on a sermon from Joseph Prince, who was talking about the first formation. From my memory, his opinion was, "Balaam could not curse the nation of Israel, because you cannot curse a cross."

Here is some of the symbolism I saw:

- The position of the tabernacle is the same position as the heart of Jesus on the cross, even slightly off-center.

- The tabernacle was at the heart of the nation of Israel, literally and spiritually.

- Balaam could not curse the children of Israel, for he was looking at a cross in the wilderness.

In the second census, the ratios of north to south, east to west have an almost equal result of 1.46/1.47. I do not fully understand the significance of the miracle seen in this ratio. Suffice it to say I am frankly amazed that after the bloodshed, deaths, and maturation of children, the north-south, east-west ratio is almost equal.

A set population of people is taken from Egypt and counted. They wander around in the wilderness for forty years, have children, their children grow up, and the generation that left Egypt dies, so after the population expansions and contractions of the tribes, we have an equal ratio? This too is of great mathematical importance and shows the hand of God was involved in the tribes.

On the last census, I used the same concept as the first, except this time, I believe the tribes were in the formation of a square to show us another mystery.

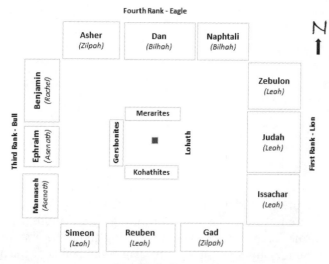

In sermons I have heard pastors relate the children of Israel's journey in the wilderness to the Christian life—the ups and downs, the struggles of this life, and a tendency toward only looking ahead to the Promised Land. Staying on this theme, herein lies the significance in what I believe God is showing us in the formation of the tribes in the two censuses.

Christianity, the wilderness, begins with Jesus dying on a **cross** and being buried and raised again. It ends with the New Jerusalem, as seen by John in Revelation. Likewise, the children of Israel began their journey in the formation of a cross and ended in the formation of a square, representing the New Jerusalem, before they go into the Promised Land.

Now that we have worked on assigning the tribes to the patterns seen in the constellations, how is this significant relative to the layout in the wilderness?

Assigning the constellations and images used on the banners for each triad provides a special setup for the tabernacle. Write down the patterns of the constellations you found for these four key tribes: Ephraim, Reuben, Judah, and Dan.

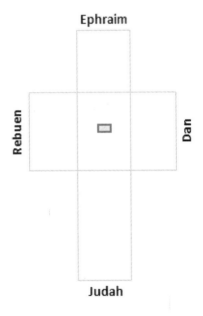

Do you recognize anything important about these four images, with God at the center? Read Ezekiel 1:10 and Revelation 4:7. From these passages, you will see the reason the last pattern of Dan, as described by Balaam, was of the utmost importance.

In case you may have made a mistake in your assignments, Ephraim was an ox; Reuben, a man; Judah, a lion; and Dan, an eagle. Surrounding the tabernacle and God were four images on the banner:

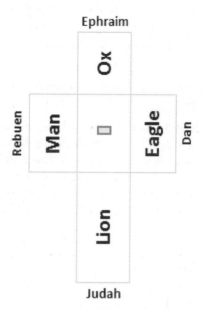

Deciphering the constellations you assigned to the tribes, remember there were four key tribes. The tribes are grouped in triads under the standards of Judah, Reuben, Dan, and Ephraim, and provide the symbolism that God would make His dwelling place on Earth similar to His throne room.

When God said "let there be light" and created the stars, He placed them in patterns so that in the future, while He was residing on planet Earth, His tabernacle would be similar to His throne room. The following passage from Isaiah 46:10 represents what we are observing:

"Declaring the end from the beginning, and from ancient times the things that are not yet done, saying, My counsel shall stand, and I will do all My pleasure."

God gave great detail to the tabernacle where He would reside, so Jewish rabbis believe the banners were also of significance. The rabbis supporting this suggest the banners that would surround the tabernacle are the same as seen in God's throne room by Ezekiel.

Ezekiel gets a glimpse of both the throne room of God and the four beasts around the throne. From Ezekiel 1:10,

"As for the likeness of their faces, they four had the face of a **man**, and the face of a **lion**, on the right side, and they four had the face of an **ox** on the left side; they four also had the face of an **eagle**" (emphasis mine).

John also will get a view of the throne room, as noted in Revelation 4:7:

"And the first beast was like **a lion**, and the second beast like **a calf**, and the third beast had a face as **a man**, and the fourth beast was like a flying **eagle**" (emphasis mine).

In discussing the special signs drawn on the flags of the tribes, Abraham Ibn Ezra, a Spanish rabbi who lived between 1089 and 1167 AD, taught:

"Our early sages taught that the banner of Reuven featured the figure of a man, symbolizing the deeper meaning of the 'dudaim'; the flag of Yehuda had the picture of a lion, for that was the image that Yaakov used to describe him; the flag of Efraim showed an ox, since he was the 'eldest of an ox;' and the flag of Dan was decorated with the picture of an eagle. THUS THEY APPEARED LIKE THE KERUVIM SEEN BY THE PROPHET YE-CHEZKEL."[55]

Expanding on the theme of the importance of the four constellations used in the banners, we also see them in the four corners of the visible heavens. At one time, these four constellations (or their boundaries) contained the Four Royal Stars of the Babylonians for north, south, east, and west. As such, they provide a further interpretation of Psalms 19:1–5.

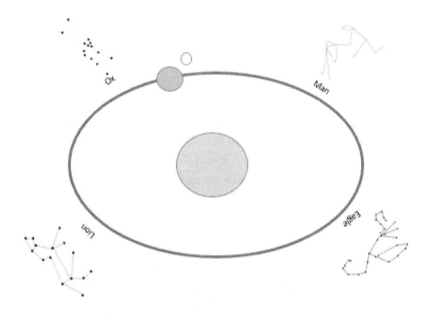

From the psalmist, Psalms 19: 1–5 (NKJV):

"The heavens declare the glory of God; and the firmament shows His handiwork.
Day unto day utters speech, and night unto night reveals knowledge. There is
no speech nor language where their voice is not heard. Their [the heavens, stars]
line is gone out through all the earth, and their words to the end of the world. In
them hath **he set a tabernacle for the sun**" (emphasis and brackets mine).

Mazzaroth the Clock

So far, we have seen three aspects to the Mazzaroth—how it could relate
to the four seasons during the year; the relationship with the constellation
Aries and the Passover; and finally, how it may relate to the constellations
of the twelve tribes, the tabernacle, and the four corners of the visible universe.

The last relationship I want to share will tie all of this together. I had struggled with this last part being real, and I may have a harder time convincing
myself than you. I do not think this is coincidental, but I will present the
evidence and allow you to make the determination. When God created
those bright shining lights, did He place them along with the position of
the equinoxes to be for markers in history, further proving He knew the
end from the beginning?

To alleviate my concerns about this being real, I reviewed this theory with
fellow Christians, elders of my church, and some pastors of different religious beliefs. I have also been able to discuss this with those of the Jewish
and Muslim faiths. I believe another outcome of this book provided me
enough information and knowledge to share my witness of how God has
worked in my life to non-Christians, Jewish, and Muslim people. The last
part of my study on the Mazzaroth applies to something I saw when studying the precession of the axis and my biblical timeline.

Taking this a step further, I broke down the Hebrew word "Mazzaroth"
esoterically. The Hebrew letter *Mem* suggests revealed knowledge of God.
Zayin connotes movements of time or completion. *Resh* speaks of leading,
and the *Tav* is indicative of a mark or sign. According to this method, the
Mazzaroth leads the movement of time through markers or signs, revealing knowledge about God and the completion of His plan.[56]

We have seen how the constellations can have multiple patterns and how
some of those patterns are found in the Bible. We only needed to get inside the head of three individuals and imagine what they interpreted in the
night sky as it related to the tribes.

As we have seen, the position of the equinoxes and solstices to the fixed stars changes over time. Applying the dates with the location of the equinoxes to the backdrop of the constellation boundaries, I saw the drift of the equinoxes over time could be representative of a clock. Not

an accurate clock per se, but as an indicator of God's **seasons**.

Using our model for the twelve constellations, I marked the first and last year the equinoxes touched the established boundaries of the constellations over the past six thousand years. Keep in mind it takes the equinoxes seventy-two years to shift one degree. I used the defined boundaries of the IAU as opposed to the stars of the constellations. I felt if I used stars, I could pick and choose a star to make it fit. For this reason, I used the established boundaries.

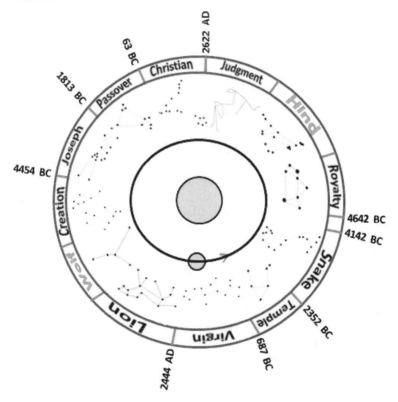

What does this tell us?

Point 1, 4454 BC. This was the last time the spring equinox was in the boundary of the constellation of Gemini, the twins. The Sumerians referred to this constellation as brother and sister. My timeline shows the creation of Adam at 4396 BC. One could correlate Adam and Eve as brother and sister—or even twins—for Eve was the product of Adam's rib.

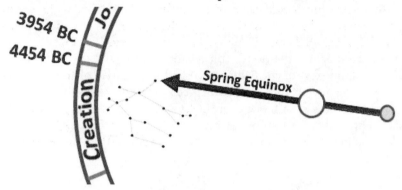

On the opposite side, the autumn equinox is in the Ophiuchus constellation, described by Jacob as a rider falling backwards. In Hebrew, the word used for backwards can also be translated as evil brother. Does this symbolize the fall of man? The next constellation the autumn equinox enters was a snake as described by Jacob, symbolizing the sin era or a symbol for Satan with the fall of man. Also take note that Ophiuchus has historically been identified as a serpent holder.

Point 2: 3954 BC to 1813 BC. We saw biblical references for Joseph being a bull, which his life absolutely was in the latter part of the Taurus "Bull" constellation. The bull was also a highly regarded animal in Egypt, which played multiple roles in this time period. On the night of the Passover, even the firstborn of cattle were killed.

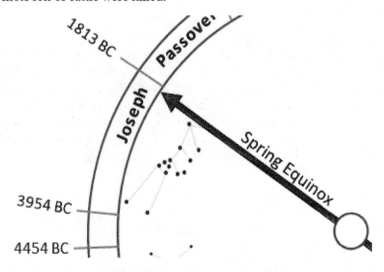

Point 3: 1813 to 63 BC. This marks the time period the spring equinox was in the constellation Aries, the lamb. As the children of Israel are preparing to leave Egypt (in 1726 BC, from my timeline), God begins a Feast called Passover, symbolized by a lamb. Do you find it coincidental the spring equinox and the day of Passover were in the constellation identified by a lamb during the time period before Christ, the Passover Lamb?

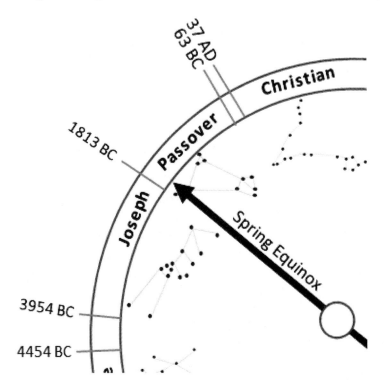

On the opposite side, the autumn equinox was in the constellation Libra, which we call wages. When my son saw this constellation, he said it looked like a tent, and I went as far as to say it could look like a temple. Analyzing photos of mosaics from 5 BC in the synagogues in Israel, I found their drawings of the temple to be similar to the Libra constellation. However, I have never seen any civilization call this a tent or temple or any building structure, but look what happens next.

Point 4: 687 BC. As the autumn equinox is leaving the Libra constellation for wages, the first Temple was "shortly" destroyed thereafter, in 586 BC

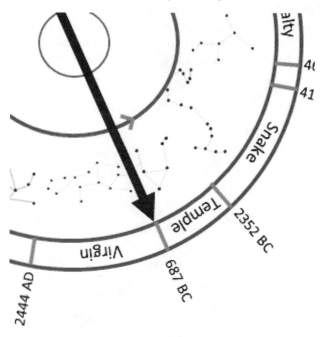

Point 5: 63 BC. I found this spectacle the most intriguing of all. As the spring equinox is leaving the Aries constellation identified with the Passover, THE PASSOVER LAMB was born.

On the opposite side, the autumn equinox was in a constellation identified as a virgin, Virgo. Before the time of Christ, the Greeks called this constellation a virgin holding a **branch!** Even though I consider Greek mythology as pagan, God was still involved, and I find it astounding this constellation is identified as a virgin holding a branch. Some even identify the branch as a palm branch. Others consider Virgo a virgin holding an infant.

> "Behold, the days are coming," says the Lord, "That I will raise to David a **Branch of righteousness**; A King shall reign and prosper, And execute judgment and righteousness in the earth."
>
> —Jeremiah 23:5 NKJV (emphasis mine)

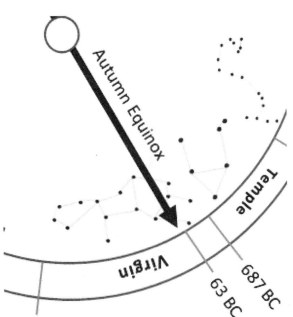

I mentioned I used the boundaries from the IAU, but in this case I looked at the main stars in Aries and Pisces. There is a gap between the two constellations from 63 BC to 37 AD; again, coincidentally, Jesus' life on Earth was during this period of time. Coincidentally, around 63 BC the Romans take control of Jerusalem.

Point 6: 37 AD. What comes after the Passover season? A constellation identified as two fish. This is the oldest symbol for Christianity,[57] which has been reduced to a single fish, and it's also where the spring equinox currently resides. The Pisces constellation marks the "season" for the Gentile and the era for Christianity.

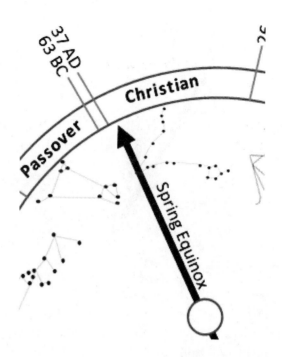

"I will keep You and give You as a covenant to the people, as a light to the Gentiles,"

—Isaiah 42:6

On the opposite side, the autumn equinox remains in the constellation for a virgin. Please note the size of Virgo compared to the others, which may mark the beginning of prophecy for a virgin to give birth and also be another symbol for Christianity. When talking with others, I sometimes identify the correlation between Virgo and Pisces as "a virgin brings in the Christian era."

"Now a great sign appeared in heaven: a woman clothed with the sun, with the moon under her feet, and on her head a garland of twelve stars. Then being with child, she cried out in labor and in pain to give birth."

—Revelation 12:1-2

To support the theory of Pisces marking the Christian era, the early Christians used the markings of two fish tied together as markers for burials to identify the dead as Christians,[58] yet avoid persecution for their faith. This fish symbol can be found throughout the Roman catacombs.

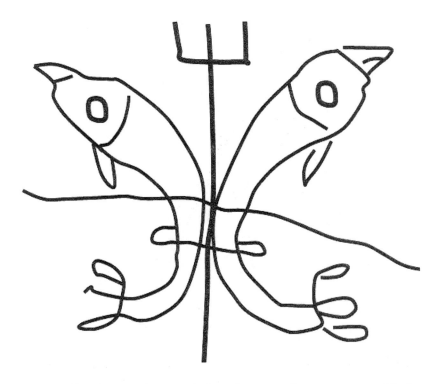

Point 7. Still with me? The next shift in the constellations occurs with the autumn equinox, as it will enter into a constellation identified as a lion (for the tribe of Judah) and the lineage of Christ. The first time the autumn equinox will enter the Leo constellation is in 2444 AD. I believe this constellation is an indicator for the return of THE GREAT LION, Jesus.

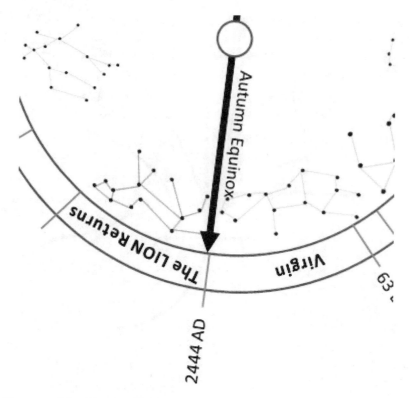

"But one of the elders said to me, 'Do not weep, Behold, the **Lion** of the tribe of Judah, the Root of David, has prevailed to open the scroll and to loose its seven seals.'"

—Revelation 5:5 (emphasis mine)

On the opposite side, the spring equinox will move into a constellation identified as water in 2622 AD, which I believe represents judgment.

Does this mean we can predict when the return of Christ will be? Not really, for we are using man-made boundaries and the equinoxes. Plus, consider the size of the sun from Earth's perspective with the stars and the slow movement caused by the precession. Do you use the first time the sun touches the boundary, the middle of the sun, the last edge of the sun, or do you use the middle of the constellation? The difference can be measured in decades and centuries.

Some call the position of the spring equinox with respect to a constellation an "age." I am not fond of the use of the word in today's language, for I think of the term "New Age." Sometimes the word "age" is used to mark a long period of time, and I find it amusing Jesus speaks of ages for eras or seasons. Look at the following passages. To what age was Jesus referring, the age of mankind since creation, the Gentile/Christian age?

"Therefore as the tares are gathered and burned in the fire, so it will be at the **end of this age**."

—Matthew 13:40 (emphasis mine)

"The enemy who sowed them is the devil, the harvest is the **end of the age**, and the reapers are the angels."

—Matthew 13:39 (emphasis mine)

"So it will be at the **end of the age**. The angels will come forth, separate the wicked from among the just,"

—Matthew 13:49 (emphasis mine)

"Jesus answered and said to them, "The sons of **this age** marry and are given in marriage."

—Luke 20:34 (emphasis mine)

When I first saw the autumn equinox entering into the constellation of a lion, I was a little depressed and questioning myself. I have always been told (and sometimes feel) we are in the "last days"; however, if the equinoxes are an indicator as this study strongly suggested, we still may be centuries away!

After pondering over this, I began thinking back to the ancient Hebrew calendar and realized it had no reference to the equinoxes. The calendar appears to have been kept in sync with the equinoxes by the adjustments for the Feast of Firstfruits.

Previously, I described a variety of symbolic references for the Hebrew calendar and month seven, which is near the autumn equinox. What if we use the position of the sun with the Feast of Trumpets as a marker?

The Feast of Trumpets currently oscillates from year to year between the constellations for a virgin and the lion, meaning we may already be in the "season" for Christ's return! (We do not need the stars to tell us this, but it's entertaining to see the symbolism in the night sky.)

If these signs in the heavens are markers for God, the return could be as soon as today, and as far out as several hundred years. We will never be given the exact time until we see the Son of Man descending, but if you want to see how close we are in astronomical terms, here is the current position of the autumn equinox and the position of the sun for the ranges for the Feast of Trumpets.[59]

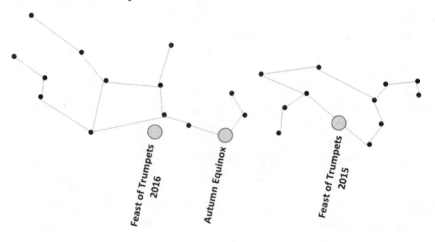

Dates for Feasts of Trumpets

Year	Day
2015	September 14th
2016	October 3rd
2017	September 21st
2018	October 10th
2019	September 30th
2020	September 20th
2021	September 8th

As I look back at all the symbolism, it gives new meaning for Jesus being called the Lion and the Lamb, represented by the symbolism of Leo with the Hebrew month seven and Aires with the Hebrew month one. Are there other "seasons" to follow? No. As I understand the prophecy for the final days of Earth, the stars will be darkened and will fall from heaven, so any alignments will also be diminished when Christ returns. This will be the end of the heavens and earth, making the way for a new heaven and new earth.

The Jewish Zodiac during the Time of Christ

In the Complete Works of Josephus, he described the design of the veil for the entrance to the Holy of Holies. I found something that stunned me, since it marked the importance of the zodiac to the Jewish people, especially the Levites who ministered before God. The veil was engraved with the signs of the zodiac. This is mysterious, for God, the Maker of the Universe, was behind the veil. We know when Christ died on the cross, the veil was torn, and we do not know the design before Josephus. The zodiac may have been added to the veil after the death of Christ.

Finally, I stumbled upon some archaeological finds of the zodiacs in the synagogues during the time of Jesus. Zodiac mosaics were found in seven synagogues, attributed to the Roman / Byzantine influence. The image that follows was found in 1920 by a farmer. This was in a synagogue by the Sea of Galilee, built just before the time of Jesus. In the center is the Greek sun god "Helios," with the temple in top of the picture; Abraham and Isaac, left bottom; and Moses and the burning bush, right bottom.

I find it amazing that Jesus may have entered theses synagogues during his ministry and taught.

Fig. 58 Hazut, Jack Beit Alpha Synagogue 0009. Source: Jack Hazut, Digital Image, Available from Israeli Image.net, www.Israeliimage.net. January 20, 2016.

In addition to the synagogue in Beth Alpha, the zodiacs appear in synagogues at Hammath Tiberias, Khirbet Susiya, Yafia, Sepphoris, Beth Shean, Husifa, and Na'aran, all constructed around 5 BC.

Look at the representation of the temple and compare it to the formation of the Libra constellation, then review point four of the "clock."

Hamat Tiberias

Fig. 59 Hazut, Jack Hamat Tiberias Synagogue 0001. Source: Jack Hazut, Digital Image, Available from Israeli Image.net, www.Israeliimage.net. January 20, 2016.

Shortly after the nation of Israel returned to their homeland in 1948, a synagogue was erected in Akko, Israel, built in 1950. The top of the dome has the same image from Beit-Alpha, and below, on the walls leading up to the dome, are illustrations of the banners of the twelve tribes. This time, the sun god Helios is left out.

Shortly after the nation of Israel became a state, it issued postal stamps with the signs of the zodiac. It appears the zodiac has been an important part of Jewish history and culture, where it may have been derived from the Mazzaroth.

Summary

Let me personally congratulate you on making it to the end and allowing me to share with you the results of my Bible study, experiences, and what has been shown to me. Great amounts of time in study, research, prayer, drawing models, artistic works, and discussions have been spent on this book.

Prior to writing this book, I had never talked to a Jewish person about faith and had never met a Muslim except from behind a counter in a store. As I finished up this book, I had two Divine appointments with two Jewish persons and two Divine appointments with two Muslims, who are now friends. If they are reading this, I hope they understand how the Divine was used in our meetings and discussions. I appreciated the open dialogue we had, and sharing our personal experiences and relationships with God. Only God could have orchestrated the series of events which took place for us to meet.

I believe God has purposed this study to provide me with an interesting topic and an approach for sharing my faith with others, even non-Christian religions. The next "season" I showed with the last part of the Mazzaroth actually lines up with the religions of Christianity, Judaism, and Islam. For Christians, the next season is the return of Christ; for Jews, the return of the Messiah; and for Islam, my friends told me the return of the prophet Jesus, who will judge the earth. All three religions are expecting a return of the same person or being.

I have shown some of the possible explanations for the Mazzaroth from the physicality of the stars, but on an internal and spiritual level, the phrase, "bring forth Mazzaroth in his season" takes on a new meaning—a deep and personal meaning that one can only understand as knowledge is obtained in asking, seeking, and knocking. I gained countless experiences in writing this book. The stars are a cool part of the Bible, but the stars were just a small part of the outcome.

Through this study, I increased my knowledge of God and the Bible exponentially. Yet I'm hesitant to say I know anything at all, for as my knowledge abounded, I feel I know less today than I thought I knew yesterday, and I understand tomorrow will show me how little I know today.

The physical side of the Mazzaroth may have many meanings, and I may have missed it completely; however, for an individual learning about God, I feel the Mazzaroth has a special, personal, and spiritual meaning for me. I believe you and I are the Mazzaroth and the season; the season represents learning about God and his ways. If the Mazzaroth were indeed a dead-end word with a lost meaning, I would have not attempted all the work and research that showed me innumerous aspects of the Bible, nor would I have learned the Old Testament enough to discuss the Bible with Jews and Muslims and share my faith with them.

To put myself in the position of Job, "Can I bring forth Mazzaroth, revealed knowledge of God, in his season?" or can I speed up the learning process and the experiences of God in its season?

Appendix I

How I Assigned the Constellations to the Tribes

Reuben

Reuben's constellation is one of the easiest to identify, for his constellation is a star pattern of a man pouring out water, today called the Aquarius constellation.

Simeon

In looking at constellations making up the two fish, one can see two swords. The Pisces constellation is one of interest to Christians, for it has been suggested as an origin for the symbol of a fish Christians use today. Others say the fish symbol is derived from Jesus feeding the five thousand with two fish and five loaves. During the time of Jesus, the Jewish people knew this constellation as two fish united.

In this instance, it appears Jacob is using swords to remember Simeon and Levi's act of cruelty with swords against Shechem and Hamon. I pictured Pisces as the depiction of swords united. Reading into Jacob's blessing further, Jacob sees a secret assembly in the future for the plot to kill Jesus.

Levi

Some give the tribe of Levi the image of the ephod on their banners, but I do not believe this is the ensign Jacob gave to the tribe of Levi. Looking through the twelve main constellations, both Gemini and Pisces have two objects joined together: two people, Gemini, and two fish, Pisces. Simeon has been assigned Pisces, and looking at the star groupings in Gemini, I saw something different in the Gemini constellation, which may fit for Levi, as found in Balaam's blessing.

Continuing on with the theme that Gemini represents Levi, is it coincidence that the current Hebrew word for the Gemini constellation is Thaumim, which translates **the united**? In English, this word is also similar to Thummin, which translates "perfection." The Gemini constellation is commonly shown with two stick people united, but I also noticed a different pattern, a pattern very familiar with the Jewish people today: the Star of David.

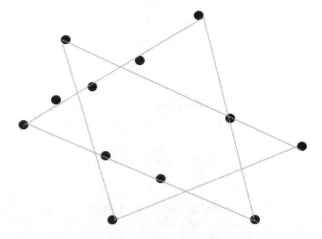

In taking a picture of the night sky of Gemini, I wanted to see if the stars in the Gemini constellation that make up the star pattern were visible. Here is the photo:

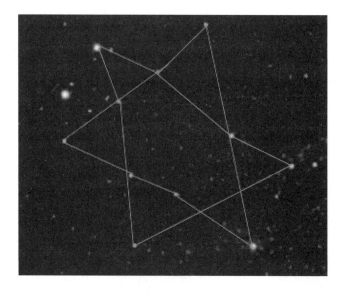

This appears to be the Star of David, but one could argue I left out one of the brightest stars in this constellation. In accordance with Balaam's theme, the unconnected star *does* look like a star rising out of the larger connected stars. I made other similar drawings including this star, called Castor, which also formed a Star of David, but it was not as distinct. I also tried drawing the Star of David in the other eleven constellations, for the Babylonians identified the pattern in Taurus as a star. I could not get a combination of stars to work in Taurus or in any other of the remaining twelve constellations. Many times in the nighttime sky, I have traced out the Star of David figure.

The Star of David has twelve points of intersection when joined by lines, and is symbolic for the twelve **united** tribes of Israel. This symbol is also known for unity. In a paper written by the faculty of Bar-Ilan University in 1998, they tell of a Yiddish anthology for the holidays that describes the unique arrangement of the Israelite camp in the formation of the Star of David.[60] According to this image, the Star of David is the symbol of **tribal unity** in Israel, a single formation protecting the sanctuary shared by all.

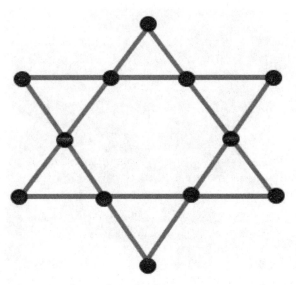

Looking at the Star of David, it clearly represents Levi being scattered in the twelve tribes of Israel. Each dot and line intersection is representative of the twelve tribes. Others also point to its twelve sides, representing each of the tribes.

In their quest for the origin of the Star of David, many believe it first appeared on the Shield of David, but where did David obtain this symbol? Since a symbolism of the name of Israel is the Power of God, it would only be fitting that its symbol would be given by God in the nighttime skies.

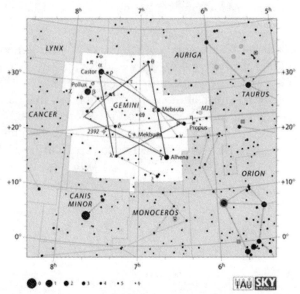

Judah

It would be interesting to count the number of times a lion is used to refer to the tribe of Judah. This too was an easy constellation assignment, for the tribe of Judah can be identified with the constellation Leo, a constellation that actually resembles its common pattern.

Dan

The constellation and pattern for Dan was the most mysterious one, for this constellation assignment was the very first one I saw when reading through Jacob's blessing:

> "Dan shall be a **serpent by the way, an adder in the path**, that **biteth he horse heels**, so that his **rider shall fall backward**."
>
> —Genesis 49:17 (emphasis mine)

As I was reading through this verse, I had the constellation of Scorpios on my computer screen and saw in the stars a snake striking the horse's heel, throwing the rider backwards. At this point, I realized Jacob was describing the patterns he saw in the night sky.

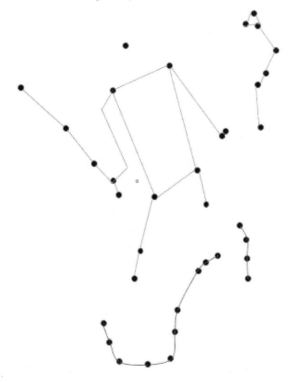

Once I realized the patterns were being described (which are not the same patterns we identify today), the other blessings began to become more coherent; however, Dan's pattern from Balaam was still a mystery. Unlocking the pattern from Balaam provided significance, as the tribes encamp around the tabernacle.

Having gone through the exercise, I knew the image I was looking for, but could never tie it biblically because it required me to know something about the habitat of the animal I was searching.

Here is the scene of Balaam. After Balaam has failed four times to curse Israel, Balak realizes Balaam cannot curse them, for he is looking directly at the tribes in a formation you will see in the encampment around the tabernacle. Balak turns Balaam away, and looking toward the Kenites, he blesses again, except it was not for the Kenites.

I had brushed over this verse many times. I thought Balaam was blessing the Kenites, yet the Kenites did not live in the rocks; they lived in the City of the Palm Trees, near an oasis in the valley of Jericho.

Later the Kenites would move and live with the tribe of Judah. Balaam was describing the habitat of the animal I was seeking, an animal making its nest in the rocks, and not the Kenites.

Before researching the habitation of this animal, I was concerned about the state of self-fulfilling prophecy, in which I would make it fit. One afternoon, I asked my wife, out of the blue, "What kind of animal makes nests in rocks?" Her reply made me laugh as I reflected on my research of the past three weeks, searching through all of Dan's blessings, Balaam's blessings, and Moses' blessing. She replied, "An eagle makes its nest in the hardest places, but hawks and condors are also known for making nests in rocks."

Sometime later, I found the following verse in Job:

> "Doth the eagle mount up at thy command, and make her nest on high? She dwelleth and abideth on the rock, upon the crag of the rock, and the strong place."
>
> —Job 39:27–28 KJV

The extensive search for an eagle will not be obvious until we complete the remainder of the tribes and look at their camping arrangement in the wilderness. Dan is an example of the same constellation having more than one pattern. This may also lead to another clue, a revealing. The tribes may not have borne physical images on their banners, but the stars of their constellation. Thus the variety of discussions and conclusions the rabbis had of the images on the tribes' banners. This may be why Jacob, Balaam, and Moses differ when blessing Dan's tribe.

The Scorpius constellation is commonly accepted as a scorpion. However, it was also perceived as serpent Jacob's blessing, and an eagle from Balaam's blessing. I could find no historical evidence of Scorpius being called a lion.

Remember that some constellation's star groupings could be used for different patterns. This is the case with Dan. Whether a serpent, basilisk, lion cub, eagle, or an eagle holding a snake, all of these images can be traced rather easily in the pattern of the constellation Scorpius.

The pattern of an eagle, with the less brighter stars:

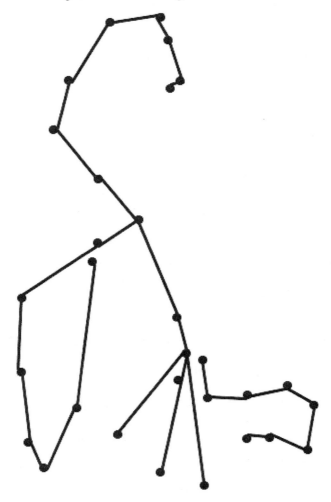

Gad

Reviewing the commonly accepted patterns for the twelve constellations along the ecliptic, the only one of a single person is Sagittarius, the archer. However, I held off assigning Gad until I had assigned the other constellations. Gad was a process of elimination, and I assigned him to Aries, the lamb.

As I studied Aries further, I learned that the Babylonians identified this constellation as a farmhand, and I had seen in a Hebrew mosaic a person drawn in Aries, which I could not locate to reference. Since I had already assigned Sagittarius to another tribe, Aries was the only one left.

Asher

"Royal dainties." I struggled with Asher much the same as I did with Gad. Actually, these two were a toss-up, for I was looking at the pattern of an archer in the skies. When I downloaded the star map for Sagittarius from the IAU's website, I noticed they did not draw out an archer, but a teapot, and the teapot actually resembled an ancient crown.

Issachar

Issachar was a fun constellation to assign. At first, I thought I had nailed this one exactly, and was amazed at how perfectly this fit. I began by breaking down the Hebrew words, trying to find an alternative meaning for Jacob's blessing. I came up with the following for this verse:

Issachar is a strong **ass** lying **stretched out** between two **burdens** [**sheepfolds**]. And he saw the **resting place** was good, and the land, that it was pleasant, so he stretched out his back to drag himself along, and became a servant unto forced labor.

Contemplating this verse's meaning and how it could relate to Christ, I pictured Christ on the cross between two thieves, burdens of society, but I couldn't quite make it fit. After a night's sleep, I woke up and searched for a star called the ass star, for burden could be a beast of burden. Lo and behold, I found the following in the Cancer constellation.

There are two stars, the **northern ass** (Arcelus Borealius) and the **southern ass** (Arcelus Australias). There's also a star cluster called M44 that the source said was **stretched out** between the two ass stars. The M44 star cluster, called *Praesepe* in Latin, means manger; it's sometimes called the Resting Place.

As I later learned, the northern ass and the southern ass stars are occasionally called the **sheepfolds**, building a bigger case for the constellation Cancer. I was excited, for I had found the perfect match for the constellation of Issachar, but there was a problem.

The star cluster M44 is not visible to the naked eye, and the naming of the other stars happened a few thousand years after Jacob. This was a situation of coincidence, and it's spooky how accurately it matches the verse in the Bible. So what constellation would you assign to wages, a tent, and a strong ass? I will have no issues if you choose Cancer.

When I showed the Cancer and Libra constellations to my son, he said they looked like tents. The constellation I assigned to Issachar is Libra, for wages. The scales are used to measure and determine the weight (payment) of something being weighed. I also noticed something else in Moses blessing, which is very short: "in thy tents" (Deut. 33:18 KJV).

Zebulun

For this constellation assignment, I had to use my imagination in the star pattern. I had seen others use the word "dwell" to assign Zebulun to Virgo, the virgin holding a branch. Dwell was referenced to the physical dwelling place of Jesus, Mary's womb. Looking at the constellation, I made out an ancient ship with a mast, a stern that curves upward, and a couple of oars. The Babylonians called this constellation a furrow, which is similar to a trench.

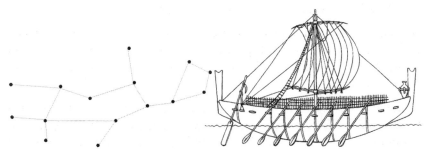

Fig. 71. Marina, *Ancient Phoenician ship*. Source: Adobe Stock. Digital Image. Available from: Adobe, https://stock.adobe.com/stock-photo/vector-illustration-ancient-phoenician-ship/64398329 (accessed February 5, 2016).

Joseph, Ephraim, and Manasseh

In Joseph's dream, there are twelve stars (constellations), representing the twelve sons of Jacob. When it came time to assign Joseph, I had in mind that both sons would share the same constellation.

I assigned Joseph and his two sons to Taurus the Bull, since he is referenced as the firstling of a bullock. In looking at the constellation of Taurus, I also saw a vine or a branch being split into two, representing Ephraim and Manasseh.

Jacob may also be referencing the constellation Pleiades as a well by the fruitful bough. Pleiades is a popular constellation mentioned in the Bible, and it is very close to the constellation Taurus the Bull. I imagined the Pleiades being a well, but I could not find a reference to a well. However, there are two stars in the Gemini constellation which have been referenced to a well by the ancients.

One Targum suggests that Moses changed the image of an ox to something else so as not to repeat the golden calf incident, but if their banners were indeed of the constellations, this would also be in line avoiding the golden calf incident. As we read later in the history of Israel, if one desires to worship something other than God, they will bring in the golden calf or whatever else is available at the time.

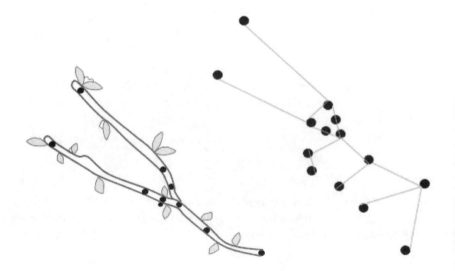

Benjamin

Since Benjamin is given two names, others have identified him with the constellation Gemini the Twins, but I offer an alternative constellation. The constellation I identify Benjamin with is the constellation Cancer. Looking at the constellation of Cancer's upside-down "Y" shape, I imagined the sitting position of a wolf howling at the moon.

The constellation Cancer is referred to as a crab, but the stars that make the shell of the crab are barely visible, if visible at all. Looking into the night, Jacob may have only seen the upside down "Y" and imagined a wolf. I have found no references to this constellation being identified as a wolf, except in a decan in Egypt, the chacal. A decan is a different group of stars within a 10° angle of the same 30° angle of the main constellation.

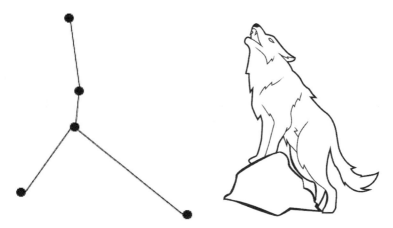

Fig. 72. Indomecy, *wolf*. Source: Adobe Stock. Digital Image. Available from: Adobe, https://stock.adobe.com/stock-photo/wolf/48875779 (accessed February 5, 2016).

Appendix II

The Golden Ratio

If the tribes of Israel were set up as a cross around the tabernacle, I thought I would find a significant ratio, a ratio found in nature, paintings, architecture, habits of people, etc. A ratio I refer to as "God's" number, also known as the Golden Ratio, the Fibonacci number sequence.[61]

The golden ratio was founded by the Italian Leonardo Fibonacci, who lived between 1170 and 1250 AD. When he was studying the breeding habits of rabbits, he found an interesting sequence and developed the following equation: $F_n = F_{n-1} + F_{n-2}$

This gives the resulting sequence of numbers: 0, 1, 1, 2, 3, 5, 8, 13, 21, 34, 55. . . . He also found that dividing a number by the following number yields a ratio, and after 8, the ratio starts approaching 0.618034 and starts repeating after 1597. Likewise, if you divide by the preceding number, the ratio repeats 1.618034.

For example, 0 /1 = 0, 1/1 = 1.0, 1/2 = 0.5, 2/3 = 0.667, 8/13 = .615, and 13/8 = 1.625

Sequence	1	2	3	5	8	13	...	1597	2584
by Previous	1	2	1.5	1.667	1.6	1.625	...	1.618034	1.618034
by Following	0.5	0.667	0.6	0.625	0.615	0.619048	...	0.618034	0.618034

Appendix III

The Marching Order of the Tribes

Judah
Issachar
Zebulun

Reuben
Simeon
Gad

Moses
Aaron

Levites with the Ark
Levites family Kohath
Levites Gershom
Levites Merari

Ephraim
Manasseh
Benjamin

Dan
Asher
Naphtali

Even though Moses was the leader, he was in the middle, perhaps five to ten miles back, so who told the tribe of Judah which way to go? As far as I understand, these people had never traveled through this land before. That leads me to believe I have stumbled upon more evidence of how God was leading the tribes by their formation.

"and that thy cloud standeth over them, and that thou goest **before** them, by day time in a pillar of a cloud, and in a pillar of fire by night."

—Numbers 14:14 KJV (emphasis and brackets mine)

Appendix IV

Excerpts from the Babylonian Talmud (Third to Fifth Century AD)

Concerning the Solar Year (Tropic of Cancer and Capricorn)

The rabbis taught: "If one comes to make a town square, he must make it as the square of the earth, i.e., the north must be towards the north of the earth, the south towards the south, and his signs shall be: **the zodiac of the capricorn** in the north and that of the **scorpion in the south**." Said R. Jose: "If he does not understand how to make it as the square of the earth, he should be guided by the equinox." How so? Where the sun rises during the long days and sets during the long days, it is north of the equator, and during the short days, where it rises and sets it is south of the equator, but during the Nissan and the Tishri equinox, it rises half (i.e., directly) east and sets half (i.e., directly) west, as it is written [Ecclesiastes 1:7]: "Going toward the south during the day, 'and turning around toward the north' during the night, 'the wind moveth round about continually,'" meaning east and west; at times it goes through them.

Concerning the Zodiac

The rabbis taught, "The sages of the Israelites assert, that **the ring (wheel)** in which the different **constellations** are situated is fixed, and every month one of the constellations appears and then recedes, making room for another, while the Gentile sages declare that the wheel is constantly turning and every month brings forth a different constellation, which is, however, fixed in its place in the wheel."

Said the rabbis (in order to contradict the Gentile sages): "We have never found the Bull in the south nor the Scorpion in the north, and were it as the Gentile sages declare, the position of the constellations would constantly change."

Concerning the Twelve Constellations

According to the sages there were twelve different constellations, one of which appeared every month, and they were as follows:

for the month of Nissan, the Ram

for the month of Iyar, the Bull

for Sivan, the Twins

for Tamuz, the Crab

for Ab, the Lion

for Elul, the Virgin

for Tishri, the Scales

for Cheshvan, the Scorpion

for Kislev, the Archer

for Tebeth, the Goat

for Shebat, the Water-bearer

for Adar, the Fishes

Appendix V

Condensed Biblical Time Line

Originally, when I created a time line for the Bible, I placed Adam and Eve in the year 4000 BC, similar to other time lines I had seen in the past, yet, when I calculated the Hebrew year, I would get 344 to 346 days in the year. The more I studied, the more confusion I had, for the Ancient Hebrews had a 360-day calendar and seemed to have systems in place to keep the year in sync with the equinoxes, or a solar year.

There are many differences and discussions on dates in the Bible, for some place the exodus at 1450 BC to line up with the name of a Pharaoh. There are archaeological findings and potential transcription errors; however, to stay core to the Bible, here is a condensed version of how I constructed a biblical time line.

Fall of Jerusalem – 586 BC

390 Years of the Divided Kingdom

Beginning of Divided Kingdom – 976 BC

      120 Years of United Kingdom

Start of United Kingdom – 1096 BC

      450 Years of Judges

Start of Judges – 1546 BC

140 Years from Joshua* to Judges (estimated) + 40 Years in Wilderness

Exodus – 1726 BC

   430 years children of Israel are in Egypt

Jacob Enters Egypt – 2156 BC

583 Years from the Flood to Jacob's Entry to Egypt

The Great Flood – 2739 BC

1657 Years of the Antediluvian Period

Creation of Adam – 4396 BC

The period after the wilderness to the Judges I have seen estimated between 7 years and 200 years. I calculated it out to be 140 years, assuming Joshua was twenty years at the time of the exodus. By some miracle, this worked out to 1,400 years between David and Abraham, as Matthew states fourteen generations between Abraham and David. Perhaps a generation for that period was 100 years?

Bibliography

1. "About the IAU," *International Astronomy Union*. Accessed July 4, 2015. http://www.iau.org/about/.

2. "Aires? Here's Your Constellation," December 2, 2015. *Earthsky*. Accessed December 29, 2015. http://earthsky.org/constellations/aries-here-your-constellation.

3. "Alexey Leonov Quotes." *AZ Quotes*. July 3, 2015. http://www.azquotes.com/author/43935-Alexey_Leonov.

4. Assyrian Clay Tablet – K8538. The British Museum, London. From: The British Museum. January 18, 2016.

5. Baum, Henry Mason. *The Church Review and Ecclesiastical Register, Volume 53*. New York: Twenty One Park Row, 1889.

6. Bentorah, Chaim. *Hebrew Word Study: Beyond the Lexicon*. Bloomington, IN: Trafford Publishing, 2014.

7. Bond, Alan and Mark Hempsell. *A Sumerian Observation of the Kofels Impact Event*. Great Britain: Alcuin Academics, 2008. Kindle edition.

8. Bouw, Gerardus D. *The Bible and the Pleiades*. Accessed July 3, 2015. http://geocentricity.com/constellations/pleiades.pdf.

9. Braganca, Pedro. "Astrology: Why Your Zodiac Sign and Horoscope Are Wrong." *Live Science.* October 23, 2007. Accessed July 3, 2015. http://www.livescience.com/4667-astrological-sign.html.

10. Burnham, Jr., Robert. *Burnham's Celestial Handbook, An Observer's Guide to the Universe Beyond the Solar System.*" Mineola, New York: Dover Publications, 1978.

11. Cain, Fraser. "What Is Tidal Locking?" *Universe Today.* November 17, 2015. http://phys.org/news/2015-11-tidal.html.

12. Cohen, Gabriel H. "How Fair Are Your Tents, O Jacob," lectures on the Torah Reading by the faculty of Bar-Ilan University, Ramat Gan, Israel, 1998. March 23, 2015.

13. http://www.biu.ac.il/JH/Parasha/eng/bamidbar/coh.html.

14. "Eclipses of 2015." NASA Eclipse Website. Accessed July 3, 2015. http://eclipse.gsfc.nasa.gov/eclipse.html.

15. Emerson, Ralph Waldo. "Nature." Boston: James Munrow and Company, 1836. Kindle edition.

16. Etheridge, J. W. *The Targums of Onkelos and Jonathan Ben Uzziel on the Pentateuch (Volume 1).* London: Longman, Green, Longman, and Roberts, 1862.

17. Etheridge, J. W. *The Targums of Onkelos and Jonathan Ben Uzziel on the Pentatech Leviticus, Numbers, Deuteronomy,* London: Longman, Green, Longman, and Roberts, 1865.

18. Flavius, Josephus translated by William Whiston. *Josephus Flavius Complete Works and Historical Background.* London, Ontario, Canada: Attic Books, 2008. Kindle edition.

19. Gaster, *Chronicles of Jerahmeel,* London: Royal Asiatic Society, 1899. Kindle edition.

20. Hillel ben David, "The Order of the Tribes of Israel." Accessed January 18, 2016. http://www.betemunah.org/tribes.html

21. "Gezer Calendar." *Jewish Virtual Library.* Accessed September 24, 2015. http://www.jewishvirtuallibrary.org/jsource/judaica/ejud_0002_0007_0_07263.html.

22. Indomecy, wolf. Source: Adobe Stock. Digital Image. Available from: Adobe, https://stock.adobe.com/stock-photo/wolf/48875779 (accessed February 5, 2016).

23. Hazut, Jack Beit Alpha Synagogue 0009. Source: Jack Hazut, Digital Image, Available from Israeli Image.net, www.Israeliimage.net. January 20, 2016.

24. Hazut, Jack Hamat Tiberias Synagogue 0001. Source: Jack Hazut, Digital Image, Available from Israeli Image.net, www.Israeliimage.net. January 20, 2016.

25. "Jewish Biographies: Nobel Prize Laureates," *Jewish Virtual Library.* Accessed December 29, 2015. http://www.jewishvirtuallibrary.org/isource/Judaism/nobels.html.

26. "Jewish Calendar." *Judaism 101.* Accessed July 3, 2015. http://www.jewfaq.org/calendar.htm.

27. Lectures on the Torah Reading by the faculty of Bar-Ilan University Ramat Gan, Israel Parashat BeMidbar, 1997.

28. Livio, Mario. *The Golden Ration: The Story of PHI the World's Most Astonishing Number.* New York: Broadway Books, 2002.

29. Marina, Ancient Phoenician ship. Source: Adobe Stock. Digital Image. Available from: Adobe, https://stock.adobe.com/stock-photo/vector-illustration-ancient-phoenician-ship/64398329 (accessed February 5, 2016).

30. Markel, Howard. "The Real Story Behind Penicillin." *PBS Newshour.* September 27, 2013. http://www.pbs.org/newshour/rundown/the-real-story-behind-the-worlds-first-antibiotic/.

31. Rav Yonatan Grossman, "How Good are your Tents Ya'akov." Accessed May 23, 2015. http://etzion.org.il/en/topics/bamidbar-0.

32. Rayburn, Stephen. "D'var Torah: Bamidbar." Accessed July 31, 2015. http://kehillatisrael.net/docs/dt/dt_bamidbar2.html.

33. Redshift, The Astronomy Software, Redshift Premium 8.2, 2014, www.redshift-live.com.

34. Rich, Tracey R. "The Jewish Calendar: A Closer Look." *Judaism 101.* Accessed July 3, 2015. http://www.jewfaq.org/calendar2.htm.

35. Richards, E. G. *Mapping Time.* New York: Oxford University Press, 1998.

36. Rolleston, Frances. *Mazzaroth or, The Constellations.* London: Rivingston, Waterloo Place, 1862. Kindle edition.

37. Seiss, J. A. *The Prophetic News and Israel's Watchman.* London: S. W. Partridge & Co., 1883.

38. Sessions, Larry, and Deborah Byrd "Aldebaran is the Bull's fiery eye." *Earthsky.* December 29, 2014. Accessed July 2, 2015. http://earthsky. org/brightest- stars/aldebaran-is-taurus-bloodshot-eye.

39. "Solar System Exploration." 2015. *NASA.* Accessed July 3, 2015. http:// solarsystem.nasa.gov.

40. Stern, David H., editor. The Complete Jewish Bible. Clarksville, MD: Jewish New Testament Publications, 1998.

41. Strong, James. *Strong's Expanded Exhaustive Concordance of the Bible.* Nashville: Thomas Nelson, 2009.

42. "The Constellations." *International Astronomy Union.* Accessed August 6, 2015. http://www.iau.org/public/themes/constellations/.

43. "This Day in History—April 1." Accessed July 4, 2015. *History.com.* http://www.history.com/this-day-in-history/april-fools-tradition-popularized.

44. Thurston, Hugh. *Early Astronomy.* New York: Springer-Verlag, 1994.

45. "NASA Eclipse Website." 2015. *NASA.* Accessed July 3, 2015, http:// eclipse.gsfc.nasa.gov/eclipse.html.

46. Wilson, Ralph F. "Early Christian Symbols of the Ancient Church from the Catacombs." *Jesuswalk.* Accessed September 2, 2015. http://www. jesuswalk.com/christian-symbols/.

Notes

1. Ralph Waldo Emerson, "Nature" (Boston: James Munroe and Company, 1836), Kindle edition.

2. *Merriam-Webster Dictionary*, s.v. "constellation," accessed August 8, 2015, http://www.merriam-webster.com/dictionary/constellation.

3. Hugh Thurston, *Early Astronomy* (New York: Springer-Verlag, 1994), 2.

4. Alan Bond and Mark Hempsell, *A Sumerian Observation of the Kofels Impact Event* (Great Britian: Alcuin Academics, 2008), Kindle edition.

5. "About the AIU," *International Astronomy Union*, accessed July 4, 2015, http://www.iau.org/about/.

6. Ibid.

7. Ibid.

8. James Strong, *Strong's Expanded Exhaustive Concordance of the Bible* (Nashville: Thomas Nelson, 2009), s.v. "Ayish," "Kaciyl," "Kaciyli," Kimyah."

9. "The Constellations," International Astronomy Union, accessed August 6, 2015, http://www.iau.org/public/constellations/.

10. E. G. Richards, *Mapping Time* (New York: Oxford University Press, 1999), 51.

11. Bond and Hempsell, *Sumerian Observation,* Kindle edition.

12. Ibid.

13. Ibid.

14. Gerardus D. Bouw, "The Bible and the Pleiades," accessed July 3, 2015, http://www.geocentricity.com/constellations/pleiades.pdf.

15. Thurston, *Early Astronomy,* 64, 66.

16. Frances Rolleston, *Mazzaroth, or The Constellations* (London: Rivingston, Waterloo Place, 1862), Kindle edition.

17. David H. Stern, ed., *The Complete Jewish Bible* (Clarksville, MD: Jewish New Testament Publications, 1998), s.v. "Mazzaroth."

18. Strong, *Strong's Concordance,* s.v. "eth."

19. Ibid, s.v. "Mow'ed."

20. Bond and Hempsell, *Sumerian Observation,* Kindle edition.

21. *Jewish Encyclopedia,* "Zodiac," accessed July 31, 2015, http://www.jewishencyclopedia.com/articles/15277-zodiac.

22. Robert Burnham, Jr., *Burnham's Celestial Handbook, An Observer's Guide to the Universe Beyond the Solar System,"* (Mineola, New York: Dover Publications, 1978), 1468, 1658, 1807.

23. "Alexey Leonov Quotes," *AZ Quotes,* accessed July 3, 2015, http://www.azquotes.com/author/43935-Alexy_Leonov.

24. *Encyclopedia Britannica,* s.v. "solar year," accessed July 2, 2015, http://www.britannica.com/science/solar-year.

25. Ibid., "Precession of the Equinoxes," accessed July 2, 2015, http://www.britannica.com/topic/precession-of-the-equinoxes.

26. Burnham, Jr., *Burnham's Celestial Handbook,* 1468, 1658, 1807.

27. Pedro Braganca, "Astrology: Why Your Zodiac Sign and Horoscope Are Wrong," *Live Science,* October 23, 2007, accessed July 3, 2015, http://www.livescience.com/4667-astrological-sign.html.

28. "Aires? Here's Your Constellation," *Earthsky,* December 2, 2015, accessed December 29, 2015, http://earthsky.org/constellations/aries-here-your-constellation.

29. Fraser Cain, "What Is Tidal Locking?" *Universe Today,* November 17, 2015, accessed December 29, 2015, http://phys.org/news/2015-11-tidal.html.

30. "Eclipses of 2015," NASA Eclipse Website, accessed July 3, 2015, http:// eclipse.gsfc.nasa.gov/eclipse.html.

31. Tracey R. Rich, "The Jewish Calendar: A Closer Look," accessed July 3, 2015, http://www.jewfaq.org/calendar2.htm.

32. "Gezer Calendar," *Jewish Virtual Library*, accessed September 24, 2015, http://www.jewishvirtuallibrary.org/jsource/judaica/ ejud_0002_0007_0_07263.html.

33. Strong, Strong's Concordance, s.v. "Chodesh."

34. 34. Chaim Bentorah, *Hebrew Word Study: Beyond the Lexicon* (Bloomington, IN: Trafford Publishing, 2014), 68, 92, 148.

35. Richards, *Mapping Time*, 147.

36. Josephus Flavius, trans. William Whiston, *Josephus Flavius Complete Works and Historical Background* (London, Ontario, Canada: Attic Books, 2008), Kindle edition.

37. *Redshift, The Astronomy Software* (Redshift Premium 8.2), 2014.

38. Richards, *Mapping Time*, 148.

39. Richards, *Mapping Time*, 147.

40. Josephus Flavius, trans. William Whiston, *Josephus Flavius Complete*, Kindle edition.

41. "This Day in History—April 1," *History.com*, accessed July 4, 2015, http://www.history.com/this-day-in-history/april-fools-tradition- popularized.

42. "Jewish Calendar," *Judaism 101*, accessed July 3, 2015, http//:www. jewfaq.org/calendar.htm.

43. Harold Markel, "The Real Story Behind Penicillin," *PBS Newshour*, September 27, 2013, http://www.pbs.org/newshour/rundown/the- real-story-behind-the-worlds-first-antibiotic/.

44. "Jewish Biographies: Nobel Prize Laureates," *Jewish Virtual Library*, accessed December 29, 2015, http://www.jewishvirtuallibrary.org/ isource/Judaism/nobels.html.

45. Strong, *Strong's Concordance*, s.v. "Yishra."

46. Joseph Jacobs and Judah David Eisenstein, "ZODIAC," *Jewish Encyclopedia*, accessed July 7, 2015, http://www.jewishencyclope com/articles/15277-zodiac.

47. Strong, *Strong's Concordance*, s.v. "'owth."

48. J. W. Etheridge, *The Targums of Onkelos and Jonathan Ben Uzziel on the Pentateuch (Volume 1)* (London: Longman, Green, Longman, and Roberts, 1862), 153.

49. Rolleston, *Mazzaroth,* Kindle edition.

50. J.W. Etheridge, *The Targums of Onkelos and Jonathan Ben Uzziel on the Pentatech,* Kindle edition.

51. Gaster, *Chronicles of Jerahmeel,* Kindle edition.

52. Hillel ben David, "The Order of the Tribes of Israel." Accessed January 18, 2016. http://www.betemunah.org/tribes.html

53. J. A. Seiss, *The Prophetic News and Israel's Watchman* (London: S. W. Partridge & Co., 1882), 364.

54. Rolleston, *Mazzaroth,* Kindle edition.

55. Rav Yonatan Grossman, "How Good are your Tents Ya'akov." Accessed May 23, 2015. http://etzion.org.il/en/topics/bamidbar-0.

56. Bentorah, *Hebrew Word Study,* 92, 68, 148.

57. Ralph F. Wilson, "Early Christian Symbols of the Ancient Church from the Catacombs," *Jesuswalk,* accessed September 2, 2015, http://www.jesuswalk.com/christian-symbols/.

58. Ibid.

59. Wilson, "Early Christian Symbols," http://www.jesuswalk.com/christian-symbols/.

60. Gabriel H. Cohen, "How Fair Are Your Tents, O Jacob," lectures on the Torah Reading by the faculty of Bar-Ilan University, Ramat Gan, Israel, 1998,March 23, 2015, http://www.biu.ac.il/JH/Parasha/eng/bamidbar/coh.html.

    Mario Livio, *The Golden Ration: The Story of PHI the World's Most Astonishing Number* (New York: Broadway Books, 2002), 96–97.